*Birthing the M*

# COSMIC
# CHOCOLATE
# ORGASM

Heartfelt Publishing PMA

*Cosmic Chocolate Orgasm* is a compilation
of previously published articles by Jayem,
together with selected teachings by Jeshua,
quotes, poems, and other inspirations
from the extensive material and practices
of the Way of Mastery PathWay.

WAY *of* MASTERY
www.wayofmastery.com

Published by:
Heartfelt Publishing PMA
PO Box 204, Ubud 80571
admin@wayofmastery.com

www.wayofmastery.com

ISBN 978-602-98911-9-5

Compiled by Raj Miles
Designed and typeset by RIS Designs
www.risdesigns.com.au

Cover art: *Out of the Ether* by Lisa McDougall
Israel photography by Nancy Lessard

*"Come! Be destroyed in Love,*
*Die into this Fire, and become*
*the Living Word...*
*arise mad lover, arise!"*

Jayem, *Recline in My Soul*

# CONTENTS: INSPIRATIONS

# CONTENTS: CHAPTERS

The way to God can only be found in your willingness
to embrace and live fully the very life that is within you,
that unfolds through you with each moment. To live
without fear, to go forward, to indeed, trust, to embrace
the very power and the majesty that is the seed, the soil,
the ground from which your life's experience is unfolding.
It is precious! It is extraordinary! It is blessed!
And it is given you of God!

*Source (1)*

# Foreword

## "Here alone do you find your true Being"

Jewels of the Christ Mind – Lesson 24

**I**t is done and it is good. Seven years of reading, studying and even teaching Jeshua's *Way of the Heart*, *Way of Transformation* and *Way of Knowing* has never managed to bring me to the personal experience of feeling the transformation required that is occurring in me right now as a result of the *Jewels of the Christ Mind* course.

These lessons skillfully crafted by Jayem to carve out a channel for the love of God to flow through me have represented my stepping stones. Each one appearing in perfection as I was ready to make the shift to embrace the next unveiling of the Truth, leading right up to this final lesson where I realize there never were any stepping stones and all that was occurring was my "Free fall into God."

How do you get to experience the Divine without someone taking you by the hand to lead you through the stages of feelings, doubts, shadows and fear? I honestly don't think it's possible to 'move through' unless a gift of this nature is offered and accepted. Thank you, Jayem for being the one with the willingness, the tenacity and the love to extend your hand and reach out to me.

Jeshua ben Joseph, otherwise known as Jesus, said,

*Awakening is not difficult.*
*You don't have to believe it.*
*You merely need to acknowledge it.*
*Each time you do so, the spaciousness*
*of your heart increases.*
*And as that occurs, the willingness to be wholly*
*vulnerable with one another will blossom.*
*And then Love can shine forth in all its glory.*
*Come to understand that when you choose to be awake,*
*you extend to the world the greatest of gifts*
*you could ever bring: the living demonstration*
*of the holy union of Father and Son.*

This book, *Cosmic Chocolate Orgasm,* has come about because of Jayem's total dedication to assisting others in their journey of awakening. I have been blessed to have spent as much time as anyone with Jayem over the past few years and have become intimately involved with the teachings, articles, poems, workshops, pilgrimages and all of the associated creativity that has birthed the PathWay, known as the *Way of Mastery.*

I feel obligated and indeed honored to share just a taste of the wealth of material with my fellow travelers. I trust that in this book we have managed to convey the Journey from the spiritual to the mystical, for it is the next step we must all take if we are to flower the soul in this lifetime. While we are all in this together, it is a solo journey – and yet, as we move together as family and friends of the heart, we find that all-persuasive strength and love which builds and expands upon itself.

To my brother Jayem who has shared his vision for the birthing of the Christ in form and bringing Heaven to Earth through this PathWay into Illumination I offer this message of gratitude on behalf of so many of us.

*'Thank you, Jayem for holding me in your heart that I might have the courage to see Myself and my Essence for what It is, I Am. For without you holding the space for me, how might I ever have known even of Its existence? I might have*

*wandered in the darkness wasting yet another lifetime. Because of you I know that this lifetime is It, that there is no purpose to my life other than to see with the fully awakened eyes of Christ and to be the Servant of God.'*

May you too, dear reader, discover the sense of wonder and feel the joyous expansion of your heart and soul as you enter this book, this compilation of the wisdom and truth of a great mystic – Jayem.

Blessings,

Raj.

~

*A Mystic Lover*

*is one who*

*embarks on*

*a profound*

*journey of*

*transformation*

*...for the love*

*of God.*

~

*Source (2)*

# Introduction

*Are you the Mystic Lover?*

*Does your heart sing for the connection to the Divine?*

*Is there but one focus in your life, a desire to return to the arms of that One that will Love you always?*

This collection of work brings a new perspective to the real meaning of life in a body. Harvested from a ripe field of spring flowers, this inspired essence of Jayem brings light to the world, revealing concepts of the Kingdom from the teachings of Jeshua and the wisdom of the single mind of the Christ Council. If you are ready, the clouds over your consciousness will part to receive a breath of fresh mountain air and you will be uplifted and refreshed again and again, finding yourself imbued in the Reality of Love.

Jeshua says, "The world is diametrically opposed to the Truth of the Kingdom." This world in which we live is *for-getting* and the Kingdom, the realm of the Divine, is *for-giving*. Love or Fear, the choice in every moment is ours for the taking. Which choice do you make?

The journey of the Mystic Lover can begin right here, and this book will support you as a sturdy staff would support a pilgrim traveling over rocky ground.

This is not a book to be read once and then buried on a bookshelf. It is not an end in itself, it is a beginning. More than the enjoyment of reading inspirational messages from a brother, it offers opportunities for interaction and introspection to bring you much greater awareness of yourself.

Each article will ask you to ponder, to go inward and discover what you feel relative to the message; 'Wonder Questions' to ask of yourself abound. The poems and prayers can be read out loud, alone or with friends. The meditations are for deepening your connection to the Divine and the many gemstones of wisdom hidden throughout the pages are to be explored for remembering and for use; let them become your daily mantras.

This is one book that you will not want to share, to lend or give away. This is your travelling companion and, perhaps, your entry to a group of friends who journeyed together once before, a long time ago. These friends come together now as family with One Heart, One Purpose and One Love. Beyond these pages lies a PathWay and a Community that is truly spread across the globe... and you are made most welcome. Like a magic carpet, the Way of the Mystic Lover will give you the ride of your life into – a Cosmic Chocolate Orgasm!

Why the *Cosmic Chocolate Orgasm*? It is just what it says, the opportunity for you to dive into the arms of your One True Love and experience – perhaps for the first time – the connection that will explode you as a Mystic Lover, the Christ Awakening into this world of form.

*Beware – Love is Divine.*
*Suzanne*

# The Way of Mastery...

*begins by accepting the humility*

*that you've created quite a mess*

*within your consciousness.*

*You've created a labyrinth*

*and gotten lost within it,*

*and you don't know the way back*

*- that OF YOURSELF,*

*YOU CAN DO NOTHING.*

Source (3)

I do not live any
ordinary moments.
With each breath my
experiences are the
stepping stones laid
before me of God,
to guide me home.

*Source (4)*

# Chapter 1

# What is a Mystic?

The word 'mystic' comes from the word 'mysterium,' or, 'mystery,' so a mystic is one who has desired – somewhere in their being – to know the divine more intimately, beyond thought, beyond theology, beyond metaphysics. A mystic is one who deliberately cultivates or takes up those forms of practice that melt away what is rigid within, who cultivates this feminine receptivity and surrender; whether it be with meditation, yoga or tai chi, there are many forms that can help melt the ice.

My own journey really began in Vietnam. I was nineteen. After a particularly hellish fire fight, I had an experience. That night I was digging a foxhole, and suddenly (I now understand it was a moment of cosmic consciousness) I literally felt stretched to infinity, I lost all sense of my individual separateness, I felt I was the sunset, I was the trees, all of these things... and the next thing I knew – whoosh – I was back to being me, a nineteen-year-old soldier, holding on to a shovel, but it was pitch black, which meant I had been standing there for probably an hour, with no sense of time. I got into my foxhole, and said, "God, if there is such a thing, I have to know what you are and what all this is about." I didn't get an answer, so I went back to being an angry nineteen-year-old saying, basically, "Screw it."

Yet, I learned that any one of us, when we utter that prayer, in whatever way we do it, God is actually already replying "Okay" and begins the process of penetrating us and guiding us with a book here, a teacher there, an uncanny and timely experience there, melting away the veils ... melting away the veils, ... until we being to sense and touch the divinity of life. We begin to soften, we begin to have our "ah-hahs." Ten or fifteen, twenty years later, we go, "Oh my God, something picked me up and has been carrying me along perfectly – and I didn't even know it." That's the *shem*★ – the *wisdom of the divine* flowing from the heart of *Alaha*★, who loves to penetrate her creation and bring it ever more into intimate alignment, intimate knowing, and intimate surrender, into that sublime mystery that is infinite, that no thought can ever possibly comprehend.

There my journey began, in a pitch-black foxhole. Upon returning home, and filled with an emaciated guilt I didn't know I had, I just happened to be drawn to a philosophy class and met my first master (though it would be years before I could recognise it). Immersion in yoga, meditation, study and experimenting with the cutting edge of altered states followed, along with abysmal failure in relationships and a divorce that plummeted me into that dark sea of guilt, utterly failing for years as a father. And that landed me in a whole new world: in-depth exploration of my own developmental stages, family of origin, and eventually pre- and perinatal birth work. I learned it is in the depths of our own shadows that we must prepare the place for God to enter.

In 1987, Jeshua (Jesus) appeared to me in a field of light in my living room (see my book *The Jeshua Letters*) and under his guidance I have been forged into genuine wakefulness; I have come to this great love of God as Divine Mystery, that alone moves me and to which I am utterly surrendered in devotional service.

~

*So, a mystic is one who comes into a profoundly deep love of the Mystery we refer to as 'God.'*

~

So, a mystic is one who comes into a profoundly deep love of the Mystery we refer to as 'God.'

It's interesting that Christianity has made such an icon of Jeshua, for the following is even recorded in the Bible:

When His own disciples poured praise on Him for what He did, He said, "Don't call me good, there's only one who is good, even, God."

Actually, he spoke in Aramaic and would have said '*Alaha*,' the Cosmic Oneness, the Mystery. He taught a way of attuning to Alaha through oneness with the *Rukha d'qoodsha*. In my workshops and training I refer to this as **LovesBreath**, the One Cosmic, Holy Breath from which all Creation arises and is sustained. He was clearly saying something he considered very important to get across to them, and thus, to all of us:

'I am just a vessel as you, too, can be.'

So he refused immediately to be put up on a pedestal, and he said there was only one good, even 'God' (if we can shift away from our egocentric and anthropomorphized idea of God). You and I are created only to be a vehicle that can allow, that can discover *how* to allow, more of that flow through us, yet — and this is of extreme importance in genuine

> ~
>
> *...this is only a tiny aspect of tantra; yet I would say that sexuality, its healing and integration, is critical for any genuine awakening to occur.*
>
> ~

spirituality — *it counters a huge egoic temptation I find disturbingly seeping into many alternative and New Age forms*: we are **not** That Great One. I am equal to you, you're my brother, you're my sister ... come, come, let's go into the Mystery ever deeper. Here is a simple paradox that becomes perfectly clear in Illumination:

*There is only God, and I am not that One. Thus, my only natural direction is in devotional surrender to That One, who alone, IS.*

Enjoy spending time contemplating that!

## Within the Way of Mastery pathway, what does the term Mystic Lover refer to? Is it tantric?

Only in the real and deep meaning of 'Tantra.' Unfortunately, in the West, tantra has come to be associated with sexual healing, wild parties, and the like. But this is only a tiny aspect of tantra; yet I would say that *sexuality, its healing and integration, is critical for any genuine awakening to occur.*

The more we melt away those places of fear and resistance and woundedness, the more we open to the sublime presence of this thing that we have to call 'Love.' I don't know what else to call it. No other word works, and here it is suffusing the air all around us, and we can just take a breath and receive it any time we want; we can let God make love to us any time we want to!

So the *Mystic Lover* is one who is cultivating a way of being that is forever in love with the Mystery, which means living in wonder, never being finished, never living in a closed box. It means the willingness to both be raised in ecstacies, dancing wildly in celebration *and* to plumb the depths of darkness and despair, and to be shattered again and again; to submit to cosmic birthing, eternally, and love the 'hell' right out of every moment!

If you take up the *injunction* of the Way of Mastery, eventually you will truly move beyond fear, and discover your very Christ nature: the deep and true part of you that can embrace all of human experience, and both *see* – and bring – a very real power of spiritual Presence to all of it. Suddenly, the Biblical utterance of God becomes shockingly self-evident:

And God looked upon all of Creation and said:

*Behold! It is very good!*

## *Why is Aramaic so significant to understanding Jesus, or Jeshua?*

When Jeshua said, 'Blessed are the meek, for they shall inherit the earth,' his Aramaic language reveals something quite profound:

*Restored and fulfilled are they who make soft what is rigid within and are moved by the Rukha D'qoodsha, for their very minds and bodies will be invigorated and inspired with new purpose.*

Rather a different picture, isn't it? Rather than a platitude, or even a hopeful and obscure promise, it's about taking a kind of action, one that *changes us.*

This is a call to great vulnerability, to breathing and feeling more deeply than ever before! It is a statement of tremendous trust, a trust that is inherently feminine in nature: *I will open and be penetrated, and in my weakness be vulnerable before this Power that wants to consume me.*

So, a genuine spirituality, I feel quite strongly, is a *mystical* journey, not adherence to orthodox doctrine, or mere translation of our lives with a new belief system. You see, orthodox religion (and New Age belief systems) merely provide a *translation* for us: we interpret things with new concepts, and try to adhere to our understanding of them. But that is really that same 'old-time religion' merely wearing new clothes!

Genuine spirituality is not merely *translative*, but *transformative.* There is a very universal template through which the soul is obliged to journey as it is *transformed*, bit by bit, until a permanent *transfiguration* has occurred.

This transfiguration is the Call of Jeshua, of the Christ Path. It is the Call of The Way of the Mystic Lover.

A **Mystic Lover** is one who has submitted to this journey of 'making soft what is rigid within,' the roots of which are surprisingly deep in the land of what we don't even know we don't know. The more that unfolds in our own case, the more the peck on the cheek becomes a juicy French kiss, and finally, the soul rests in cosmic intercourse with God!

(If that pushes your buttons, just know the sediment of fundamental Christianity really does live in your cells somewhere. It's okay to relax, and want to *feel* God, not just *believe* in God!)

Such a PathWay is anathema to orthodoxy and fundamentalism in whatever religion it is found. It's always been squeezed to the edges of societies. Yet such a PathWay is clearly at the heart and soul of Christ's teachings — for example, *if* one is willing to investigate what He really taught in His Aramaic language, even if you don't trust that He is the source author of, say *A Course In Miracles*, or reject the Jeshua Teachings that have come through me, as 'merely suspect channeling.'

Personally, I am not interested in defending, or persuading. My Work is about *serving*: it is inevitable in the mystical pathway of transformation that one becomes less and less interested in anything but this great Mystery, clearly penetrating and transfiguring Humanity!

It becomes impossible *not* to be transformed into one whose heart longs to share and give what has been received. Jeshua refers to this stage as the *Way of the Servant*, and says it is both the highest and final phase possible in the field of space-time.

~

*To take up this
PathWay is to awaken
from the Great Spell.
It changes everything.
Everything!*

~

This mystical current, again, is found in all traditions. In the West, it emerges in some Gnostic texts, and is currently sweeping again more deeply into human awareness. For example, although *The Da Vinci Code* is simply a watered-down use of some intriguing information to build a scintillating fictional story, it has helped to bring into awareness the hidden current of the Feminine that is so critical in genuine spirituality.

## What's so important about the Mystical Path?

Mankind is at a huge crisis point. The effects of humanity, split off from its more feminine and mystical capacities, are clearly evident in the destruction of the biosphere, the continuation of violence and war, and the epidemic growth in neurosis.

The Cosmic Field, or *Rukha d'qoodsha* is polluted with *substitutes* for the Real Thing. We need desperately to inspire millions to seek their own direct *feeling intimacy* with Divine Mystery, for here alone is Separation overcome. *When you feel suffused in the Mystery, you know the earth is your body, and all beings your brothers and sisters.*

The way of the world is the Blue Pill. The Way of Mastery is the opportunity for the Red Pill, to use the analogy from that brilliant, archetypal film, *The Matrix.*

To take up this PathWay is to awaken from the Great Spell. It changes everything – everything! And yet, I give you warning: the one who ends such a Journey is not the one who begins it, for the self becomes a Servant of Mystery, of the Divine, even while being engaged in the struggle of eternal Birthing into even more of that Mystery.

Jeshua once said to me:

> *'It is the ego that comes first to spirituality.*
> *It believes here it will find the forms of power,*
> *the kind of peace it wants. It does not know that it is*
> *moving toward its own doom, as the illusion of the*
> *separate self is dissolved, and Christ arises in its place.'*

And as that happens, we are 'turned' more and more to being Servants, and that can be challenging. Yet, all along, from the moment we offer that first prayer – as I did in a foxhole in Vietnam – Grace has swept us up and God lives us into the answer to the deepest prayer of our soul.

### A Few Important Notes:

★ 'shem' is the Aramaic root word for 'Holy Spirit.' It refers to the infinite field of pure intelligence, wisdom, healing power available to anyone who cultivates an openness to it: a quiet mind, a willing heart, and the development of deep feeling, which can be frightening as we meet our 'shadow.' In the early Greek translations of Aramaic, 'shem' was translated as 'Sophia' (Greek goddess of Wisdom). Later, it comes to us in English as 'the Holy Spirit.'

★ 'Alaha' is the Aramaic name for the Absolute that Jeshua/Jesus would have used most often. Again, it refers to a field of Infinite Mystery that is unseen, yet pervades all Creation, and is the Source of all things. Thus, 'God' is the Self — the Impersonal Matrix of stillness, power, wisdom and Love, that underlies our 'little self,' like the depth of the ocean, underlies, allows, and supports each temporary wave that arises and dies.

★ To 'see': Mystical transformation truly makes visible what 'eye hath not seen, nor hand grasped.' Our word 'God' comes through the Latin, *deus*, which means, 'to see'! 

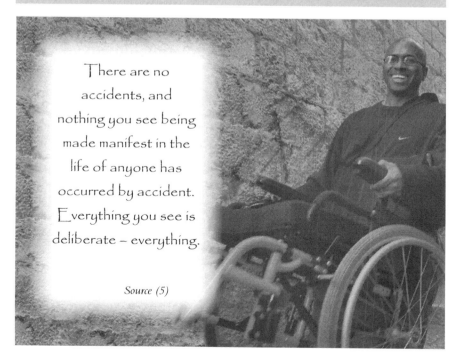

There are no accidents, and nothing you see being made manifest in the life of anyone has occurred by accident. Everything you see is deliberate – everything.

Source (5)

*What do I truly want?*

# POEM:
# Creed of the Mystic Lover

Choose the moment of Your coming, Lord.

Pierce the veils and make me Your Lover.
I will prepare this marriage bed,
smoothing the wrinkles of my mind
and dusting the corners of my soul,
then sit naked
before Your single candle flame
ravaged in this secret longing satisfied only in You.

Unless I am Yours, I am nothing.
Unless You fill me, I am empty.
Unless You are given through me, nothing is given.

Choose the moment of Your coming, Lord.
Ignite the heat of Your presence,
as I am made the fuel of Your fire.
Make me Your Lover,
and pour Yourself into this world through me
until I am destroyed in Your giving.

Then,
let me be forgotten by the world
as it gazes upon You in praise and adoration,
lost in the dancing that destroys the sorrows
holding this world too long.

Consume me in You, Lord.
This is enough.
This, is All.

*Source (6)*

Only Christ can walk in this world, yet
not be of the world. And only Christ
can transcend every limited and fearful
creation into the beautiful flower that
blossoms and gives its sweet fragrance
to all of creation. And is it not that which
you long to feel moving through your
beingness? Is not that call to awaken alive
within you? Oh, beloved friends you know
that it is!

*Source (7)*

## Chapter 2

# The Prayer of the Lord

*H*e had marveled at the unfolding of it all. His life of preparation was now bearing fruit, and all these things were signs to Him that His teaching Work was to now unfold. His old friends, cousins, family, and familiar villagers had marveled at His growing popularity. Many warned of how He 'stirred the pot,' and would make enemies. Many simply stayed away altogether.

*The mysterious, unseen, incomprehensible and infinite Light he had spent His life discovering, attuning to, and surrendering into – which He referred to variously as 'Alaha' and at times as 'abba' (to help convey that the Light had an intimate and direct relationship with each and every aspect of the Creation that sprang forth from It; that every leaf, every droplet of water, and every living soul had but one 'Father-Mother,' for 'abba' meant simply 'parent') – had shown Him these 'signs,' and now it was His time to begin.*

*He arose from His silent meditation beside His beloved Sea of Galilee, near Caperneum, and waited for the caress of dawn. There! And now, his skin began to warm. He closed His eyes, and let His breath carry the solar energy into every cell. Today would be the day. Today He would begin to answer the question they had asked of Him. And a wise teacher gives only when asked: only then is there a place in which what is given may be received. Their question was this:*

Rabbi, how do you attune to Alaha as you do,
allowing such manifestations of Love to appear?
Please, teach us to pray as you do.

*They were gathered now, the question foremost in the minds of each. He paused and looked upon them. He felt the thirst in their souls, that precious longing and willingness to learn. He raised His arms and stretched them wide, bent at the elbows, palms open heavenward, as His head tilted back, eyes closing. His body expanded as it received the Breath of Life deeply. And when He spoke, the very first word resounded and penetrated them all, as though lightning itself had struck them, their very bodies resounding in the way a gong responds to the blow of the striker. That very first word was already the answer to their request!*

*He would spend the day with them helping them to open to the practice of attuning to Hashem, the Nameless One, the Infinite Light, the Ever-Shimmering One, Father-Mother of the Kosmos, Abba.*

*And the Word that resounded from Him, the Word they began to explore, to feel, to breathe ever more deeply in rhythmic flow was:*

## *Ah-bw-oo-n!*

*Only after what must have been hours, though time had melted into timelessness as they became immersed in the feeling-practice He gave them, did He signal for them to rest and recline in the shade of the trees at the edge of the gently lapping waves that kissed the pebbles of the shore.*

*And when He spoke, every word revealed this way of prayer, what would one day come to be known as* The Lord's Prayer. *But it would be better to call it* The Prayer of the Lord, *which means 'the way of attuning [prayer] to the field of harmonious Light in which all wisdom resides [Lord].'*

*He spoke this day only three short lines, giving no indication that there would be more to this way of prayer:*

## *Ah-bwoo-n d'bwash-mahya*
## *Neeta – Kahdaasha – schmach*
## *Tay-tay mal-koo'-tha!*

That is to say:

**Father–Mother of the Cosmos (ahbwoon) spread everywhere throughout the Kosmos (d'wash-shem-ahya),**
**You penetrate us now as we dedicate our bodies as temples (qadash, to make holy)**
**and breathe Your Holy Breath! (schmach, from 'shem'),**
**and now we feel our very being becoming a fertile field for creating (mal-koo'-tha)!**

Centuries later, this marvelous teaching would become reduced through mistranslation into empty words of mere belief:

*Our Father, who art in heaven,*
*Hallowed be thy Name.*
*Thy kingdom come, thy will be done*
*on earth as it is in heaven.*

*Forgotten would be the truth that the 'earth' is one's very own bodymind, a 'fertile field' indeed when infused with the shimmering intelligence and flow of the Light, Wisdom, Power, and Vision contained in the "Name"; a sign spread everywhere, unseen, yet the field of infinite intelligence permeating all things. This was the 'Shem'!*

*The first stage of practice He gave them was within the very first sacred Word:*

## Ah-bwoon

• *'Ah' … the vibration of the All, or 'Alaha,' the name for God that Jeshua would have used often.*

• *'bw' … something is arising and wants to 'ripple' to us. The Divine desires to enter Its Creation and guide it.*

• *'oo' … the sign of the breath. The Divine is 'breathed' toward us; may the outbreath of God become our inbreath. May we return all within us to be purified and released in the infinite and loving Presence of the Divine, as our outbreath becomes God's inbreath. This is how close the Divine is to us, how intimately involved!*

• *'n' … the feeling tone of 'matter,' of the very cells of the body itself. Vibrating like ripples from a pebble tossed into a still pond.*

★★★★★

So much more than empty words, what we call *The Lord's Prayer* is actually a living practice of attunement, a *yoga*. This is what He gave them that day, what He gave all beings who would find their way to the soul of His Teachings. It is available still to those who long for more than beliefs, who long for the intimate kiss of the Divine in their own being, guiding their own life.

May all beings recover this sacred Truth, and honor our beloved Way Show-er, as it becomes the substance of their very being! May all beings be quickened, healed, and awakened to the extraordinary and marvelous and immediate feeling nature of the greatest love affair of all: that of Creator (God) and Creation (soul)!

*Thank you, sweet Brother, for returning the jewels of your Teachings to us, hidden and lost with your very own Aramaic language....*

Here alone, in this mystical 'wedding feast,' may Nature (bodymind) be transformed, expressing the living vision of extending only the *Good*, the *Holy*, and the *Beautiful*, by enjoying this immersion in this sacred attunement that the Rabbi once taught his friends. Here alone does the soul heal its anguish of alienation, of separation, and the sense of tormenting aloneness that leads to all manner of insanity plaguing humanity.

May all beings truly be helped to 'come Home,' into the actual feeling-nature of this intimate Oneness that quenches all thirst, and grants us the true peace from which we are renewed and restored to Wholeness, from which all beings may take up their rightful place as co-creators, and heaven may descend to earth.

Care to join me? Together, watch our Circle grow!

*Thank you, sweet Brother, for returning the jewels of your Teachings to us,*
*hidden and lost with your very own Aramaic language.*
*Forgive us, and teach us anew.*
*Thank you, LORD, thank you, Jeshua, thank you.*

# The Aramaic Lord's Prayer
## Attuning to the Cosmic Fire

*Ah bwoon d'bwashmaya*

**Father-Mother of the Kosmos, Ever-Shimmering Light of All,**

*Neeta kadasha schmach*

**Your Light is focussed within us as we breathe Your Holy Breath.**

*Tay tay malkootha*

**Now, you enter the sanctuary of our shared Heart,**

*Ne-whey t'savee-yanak eye kanna
d'bwashmaya opf-baraha*

**uniting within us the sacred rays of Your Power and Beauty,
awakening our heart's desire that unites heaven and earth
through our sacred Union.**

*How-lahn lachma d'soonkahnan yow-manna*

**Your Light shall guide us as we fulfill what lies within the circle
of our lives today.**

*Wash wo-klan how-bane eye-kanna dahp hahnan
shwa-ken el'high-ya-bane*

**We know that you already forgive us our secret fears,
as we choose to forgive the secret fears of others.**

*Oo-lah tah-lahn el-nees-yo-nah ella pah-sahn min beesha*

**Let us not enter forgetfulness of Reality, tempted by false
appearances.**

*Metahl dih-lah-kee mal-kootha, oo-high-la,
oo-teesh- bohk -ta. La- alahm, ahl-meen!*

**For from your astonishing Fire comes the Eternal Song
restoring and sanctifying all;
It is renewed eternally in our lives, and throughout Creation!**

*Ah-mayn.*

**We seal these words as Truth in our hearts, committed fully in trust
and faith, as together we say:
Ameyn**

*Source (8)*

*How would I feel if I were able to communicate to God in the original words of Jeshua? Am I willing to commit to learning this prayer in Aramaic by heart in the next month?*

When you have come to allow all things,
to trust all things, you will have embraced
all things. And only that one who is larger
than the thing which is embraced can do
the embracing. Therefore, whenever you
feel imprisoned, it is because you have made
yourself smaller than the world you perceive.
And when you feel free, it is because you've
remembered that you are the one from which
all things have arisen. You are the Son of God.


"My goodness, I don't have to go anywhere.
It's right here in front of me. This ordinary
moment provides the doorway to the
transformation of consciousness itself.
All I have to do is bring a little willingness to
it. And guess what? I have all power under
Heaven and Earth to do just that. Nobody can
take it from me! I am the one who can bring
that little willingness to this moment and let
the raindrops hit the window."

Source (9)

# Principles of Christ Mind

- *Only Love is Real – What is real cannot be threatened by what is not real and does not truly exist.*

- *Love requires no effort, only a little willingness necessary to allow it to flow.*

- *Therefore, The Way of Mastery does not require you to change your circumstances; it merely requires that you change your attitude toward them, by recognizing that they are harmless; by recognizing that you have called all things to yourself.*

- *Can you find a place in which you merely rest in awe, and recognise your complete ignorance?*

- *The use of time is pivotal. The use of time determines, at all levels, what you will experience in your tomorrows.*

- *There is nothing that you see that is not pervaded by the Perfect Radiance of God's Holy Presence.*

- *Your treasure is your Reality as the unlimited, holy and only begotten Child of God.*

- *A grand thing about Love: It does not require any set of conditions to exist before It does.*

- *I am free to look lovingly upon the world. I do not wait for something outside of myself to create a stimulus that elicits a loving response.*

- *Mastery comes when finally you choose to release all attachment to fear.*

- *The only choice you ever have is this: Will I assume responsibility for doing whatever I must do to eradicate every misperception, every obstacle to the presence of Love, every limited belief I have ever learned about anyone or anything – especially about myself? When will I choose to assume responsibility for cultivating the perfect remembrance that **I and My Father are One** – so that I can perceive the real world?*

*Source (10)*

The mind that allows all things, trusts all things, embraces all things – is all things. And yet, though you will seem to live, yet you will not live. But That One alone lives as you. You are free. You are vast. You are without birth and without death.

*Source (11)*

# Chapter 3

# Free Falling into God

You are a skydiver. Once upon a distant past time, I forgot that. Perhaps you have, too. There is something just a bit odd about the kind of skydiver we all are. First of all, none of us needs an airplane, and the bulky pack that contains our chute is invisible to the eye! In fact, it can't be found on our backs, but occupies a few small inches of width and depth within our skulls, and an even smaller space, there, in our hearts. Small and invisible, yes, but upon the quality of that chute literally everything which makes up our experience in life depends!

You see, we do not jump out of airplanes. We leap within the infinite Sky of Mind itself! It is a sky of unlimited possibilities, and our experience is based not just on how we have packed our chute, but on what kind of chute we have chosen in the first place.

A master Sky-of-Mind diver has discovered something of great importance.

Unfortunately, it is still a secret on our planet. It is a secret that each of us must truly embrace if mastery is our goal. Here is the secret:

The chute that feels most comfortable and familiar is one that has been made and packed for us, rarely by us!

So, the first thing a master diver does is decide to start from scratch, designing and making the chute he or she most wants to use and, if they feel it isn't quite working the way they want, they take it apart and change it.

We all emerge in this odd mystery called Existence in the same way. We emerge out of the context created by our birth parents, our society, and the time frame in which we are physically birthed. Our 'chute' is packed for us as these subtle forces begin to define the nature of the Sky of Mind for us. This includes the field of what is possible and what isn't, what is right and what is wrong, and – at the deepest level possible – what is, and what isn't! As you accepted the chute common to everyone around you, the realm of possibilities began to dwindle for you. Many people added a piece of material to your chute, and even did the sewing for you! Usually, it is not until we have had enough of feeling constrained, crashing into rock walls, and constantly missing our landing targets, that we feel compelled to examine the chute we are using!

And that is exactly the moment when the potential for mastery begins to stir within us.

The process of Enlightenment is really the act of looking within at the chute we are so accustomed to using – so accustomed that we have fallen into a common pit of quicksand: we believe we *are* the chute we are using! And, until we separate ourselves from that delusion, we will remain in resistance to examining it, and the thought of changing it will appear dreadful, indeed!

So, I want to share a fundamental axiom with you. A truth that everyone on the way to becoming a master Sky-of-Mind diver discovers:

*You are already free falling in God,*
*infinitely and perfectly safe,*
*supported unconditionally to create*
*whatever you want to experience according*
*to the chute you choose to use!*

Since this is true, the first step to Mastery is to give up complaining about the way "it" is. You know – "IT." That thing we call "reality." We think we see it, out there, but upon closer examination, we discover only our own unique chute: that thin membrane of perceptions and beliefs we may not have known were sewn together. When the wind blows through the Sky of Mind, it is our unique chute configuration that determines which way we will drift. All attraction and aversion we experience, all fear and self-doubt, and all God-realization is rooted in that tiny, invisible pack we wear within our being.

A second axiom for Masters-in-Training is this:

*You must be willing to unsew your chute,*
*and be taught how to sew anew.*

No master ever defends his chute!

A master is too interested in free falling more gracefully, successfully, and joyously, to waste time with self-defense. In short, a Master is actually just a very good and willing student, with an unceasing desire to learn anew!

The last axiom in the Book of Sky-of-Mind Divers that I will share here is this:

> *Joy is the compass*
> *by which to cultivate the*
> *sewing of your chute.*

That is very different, even radical and threatening, to those who may have been involved in constructing your first chute, the one you call "me." For Joy has nothing to do with the following, very common pieces of cloth:

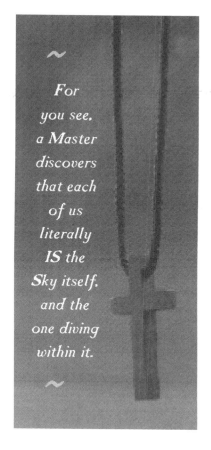

*~*

*For*

*you see,*

*a Master*

*discovers*

*that each*

*of us*

*literally*

*IS the*

*Sky itself,*

*and the*

*one diving*

*within it.*

*~*

- Pleasing others.
- Assuming responsibility for another's unhappiness.
- Sacrificing as a way to extend love.
- Working hard to earn the right to play more.
- Joining others in decreeing: "We are all victims here!"

What other statements can you discover in the 'chute' you were given?

And, in closing, I would offer you this: How do you *want* it to be?

We all have free choice in which chute to use and the potential to become master chute-makers. We do not, however, have the freedom to refrain from diving in the Sky of Mind! We have done it since before the beginning of space-time, and we will never cease doing so. For you see, a Master discovers that each of us literally IS the Sky itself, and the one diving within it...

*Specifically then, what stands between me and this goal I seek?*

# Prayers of the Mystic Lover:

## Prayer of Declaration

*When next someone asks you, "Who are you?"*
*please do not give them a name. Do not say,*
*"Well, I was born in a certain town in a certain part*
*of the planet."*
*Do not tell them that you are a Democrat, or a Republican,*
*or a Communist, or an atheist or a Catholic.*
*Tell them the Truth:*

*Who am I?*
*I am the extension of love in form.*
*I have never been born*
*and I will never taste death.*
*I am infinite and eternal.*
*I shine forth as a sunbeam to the sun.*
*I am the effect of God's love.*
*And I stand before you to love you.*

*Now that will raise some eyebrows! It will also transform your*
*world. For it is time to stop seeking Christ outside and start*
*choosing to take responsibility for being Christ incarnate.*

*Source (12)*

# Stepping Stones # 1

*When you awaken in the morning,
and you've planted your feet firmly
on your floor, take pause
and ask yourself this question:*

*What do I want right now?*

*Remember that what you decree is,
and the thought you hold in the mind will
be reflected through the nature of your
experience. So take pause and ask,*

*What do I want?*

*And then simply give yourself one minute
to observe whatever comes up in the mind,
or even is felt in the body.*

*Source (13)*

"Where you join in equality with me, our minds are joined eternally. And if two or more are gathered in my name — which is simply to be in the presence of the energy which is Christ — miracles can return to this world. And what you think of as grand impossibilities: there is no such thing."
*Source (14)*

"Love begets miracles, and miracles shorten the need for time."
*Source (15)*

"The body, then, is not a limitation and not a prison. It does not control you and of itself it carries no intelligence. It is, however, the perfect servant. What then would you have the body serve? Love or fear? Forgiveness or self-judgment?"
*Source (16)*

"Be you therefore that which you are, and you are the Light of the World."
*Source (17)*

"Where you choose Love now, you heal the past. And because all minds are joined, when you choose to teach Love now in some circumstances that before got your dander up a bit, where you teach Love now, you release everyone in the past you have ever known that shared an experience that was left unhealed."
*Source (18)*

You are the one who remains free to assume
responsibility for the domain of your mind.
You are the one who is free to simply say:
Father, nevertheless, not my will,
but thine be done.

*Source (19)*

## Chapter 4

# Interview with a Mystic Lover

### *How can a person get closer to God?*

To keep it succinct, begin in this way: bring awareness OUT of the grasping mind, by simply feeling the body as it is. Release any unnecessary tension. Then, observe the breath, and notice if it is flowing deeply, down into a relaxed belly. If it isn't, simply desire and intend for it to do so, and take whatever time is necessary to relax into a deeper flow of breath. Gently introduce the following as a quiet thought, or mantra:

a) I do not know what a single thing is, or is for. I accept my non-knowing. (Followed by a few moments of observing how this may change the breath, and re-establishing relaxed flow.)

b) I can have no existence apart from God, period. For if I were separate from That One, I would not exist. (Again, breathe.)

c) My existence is not **for** 'me.'

d) I am willing to allow God to teach me anew who I really am, and what my existence is for.

Then simply breathe, express gratitude, and allow any images, feelings, or sensations to pass through, without resistance.

You see, we do not so much get closer to God, as soften what may be rigid within *against* God's coming closer to us.

## If everything is *One*, why does everything occur as parts or pieces?

Oneness does not contradict uniqueness. Creation is, by definition, the formation of something unique. All created forms have a beginning, and an end. This includes ideas and beliefs *about* self, God, and Reality. Oneness is not known through belief, but by direct apprehension in mystical, transcendent awakening. It is *intuited,* however slightly or greatly, because it is the eternal field of Reality in which Creation occurs. Part of Creation is clearly that there is an appearance of parts/pieces. Clearly, the One must love manifesting as the Many! Thus, in a genuine spirituality, one comes to reconcile what mystics call the 'coincidence of opposites': Oneness **and** Many are embraced and lived without resistance.

~

*Spirituality is the art of cultivating and awakening latent capacities for improved 'seeing into', or penetrating, Creation itself.*

~

Sounds simple – and yet the process of healing consciousness into this generally takes a minimum of fifteen years or more from the moment one first really embraces and engages genuine spiritual practice, since it first flushes up everything obstructing this awareness! Not entirely pleasant, but entirely necessary. For example, in *A Course In Miracles*, Jesus clearly states: "It is not necessary to seek for Love, for that is what you are. It is, however, necessary to seek for what is false." And that falseness – unfortunately for our little egos – is not outside of us at all!

There is **no way** to fully and directly know Oneness except by engaging the process of 'seeking what is false,' so that its spell-binding power is dissolved. Seeking moments of ecstasy may be helpful, like a good appetizer, but such moments are not a replacement for the meal.

Actually, *nothing occurs as parts/pieces.* It merely appears that way to the degree consciousness has not matured its capacity to 'see between the lines,' or to cognize what was not previously 'seeable.' Our word for the divine, 'God,' comes from the Latin, *deus*, which literally means 'to see.'

Spirituality is the art of cultivating and awakening latent capacities for improved 'seeing into,' or penetrating, Creation itself. And, again, this occurs naturally as we take up a path of letting 'God' get closer to us, of letting the Divine penetrate us.

## What causes fear?

**F**alse **E**vidence **A**ppearing **R**eal. Fear is always the result of operating from a level of consciousness not sufficient to 'see' into the Reality of things. Ultimately, it is founded on a case of mistaken identity: ours! We believe our existence is our job, our relationship, our bank account, our 'image,' our body. We project our ignorance outward, 'seeing' parts/pieces, where there is really only Oneness occurring perfectly. Fear = the false perception that my existence is threatened, because we have not yet realized what our real Existence is, or is for. In fact, we do not generally even know Who exists, truly! Thus, ignorance generates Fear, always.

Jeshua once said, "Fear is the only energy you can be said to have created. In Reality, it does not exist." This means that whenever we are in Fear, we are nowhere! Even so, Fear is part and parcel of what glues molecules together, until mystical alchemy converts consciousness sufficiently so that Love has replaced it. Love allows all things, trusts all things, embraces all things, and is thus forever transcendent of all created things. This is what it means to be 'in the world, but not of the world.'

## How does fear arise?

Fear arises through the process of false self-identification, and becomes a habit. It is actually a 'grip' so pervasive, in almost all beings, that it will appear at the first sign of perceived threat to our self-identity. Christ said, 'the last to be overcome shall be death.' The Yoga Sutras say that fear of death is the last obstacle to enlightenment. Death of what? The only thing that can die is a thing that has been created. Yet, the True Self is not a created thing. The only thing that can interrupt the process of fear arising and taking over the party is the Remembrance of the True Self.

## How can a person release fear?

The very first step is in fully acknowledging and feeling it when it is present, so that it is not projected. If all human beings took this simple first step, there would be no war, crime, or poverty whatsoever. For the world is the result of the projection of fear, in an attempt to get rid of it! Just acknowledge it, feel it as an energy, and learn to breathe deeply in spite of it.

Fear is the only discrete energy it is impossible to change, since it is fundamental to being a bodymind in space–time. It underlies all anger, and all sadness, and all composite energy states. It is often being subtly held in place even in the attempt to be loving, and thus limits Love.

As one begins to discern spiritual truth, 'seeing' is developed. It becomes more and more evident that the presence of fear is only a forgetting of Reality. Thus one can say, "This fear cannot be real. I am willing to see this in a more loving way." Jeshua told a friend, "The most loving story is the most true." Always be willing to discover the 'most loving story,' or perception, of what is occurring. This is not simply a mental trick. When you do so, you are allowing God to penetrate your veils more deeply, and reveal more of the Light to you.

Also, when seemingly paralysed, stuck, or at the effect of fear, choose to take loving action immediately! Simply ask, "How can I extend Love right now? To whom?" For love to be extended through us, it must first be received by us! Fear is ultimately false. Just get proactive about loving, **after** you have acknowledged and fully felt and breathed with the energy of fear. Since it is a 'false god,' just get on with loving, and – in every instance – you will discover that things take care of themselves!

And so – only Love dissolves Fear. But we are habituated to the drug of attempting to get the universe to arrange itself according to what we think must happen to save us from what we fear. Death, change, loss; we fear them when, in reality, they don't exist. There is only Eternal Birthing occurring. A bird is cast from its nest only because the mother knows it is time to fly. We suffer when we refuse to extend our wings, or attempt to clip those of others.

## *Why does this reality seem to be so challenging for people?*

Reality is not challenging at all. Resisting it, is. What we usually call 'life,' challenges us because we are operating from fear and abide in Ignorance of Reality. We suffer because we are still under the delusion that we must bend and shape creation to provide our safety, and so on. But our Real Existence cannot be threatened at all.

*Only Love dissolves Fear.*

## Who is answering these questions?

If I say, "I am..." I am a liar and a hypocrite. If I say, "Another is..." I am a liar and a hypocrite.

Only when one has sufficiently taken up spiritual practice (which is what dismantles the false self) can this reply be understood.

The less there is of 'me,' the more there is of the True Self. Consider this bizarre utterance by Christ: "He who sees me, sees the Father." Yet a man was uttering these words!

A worthwhile question to contemplate would be: "Who is asking these questions?"

## What do you like about channeling?

Nothing! It's a Pandora's Box of possible self-deceit, temptation for ego aggrandizement, and – if one is humble enough with it – the call to take up the challenge of radical transformation. What's to like about that? Anyone who goes even a little way down the path of genuine spirituality knows it shatters the comforts of the false self; it does not save it! Anyone who purports to 'channel' must constantly 'test the spirits,' recognise the inherent capacity for self-deception in the ego, and recognise a profound and challenging responsibility regarding others. Whenever I encounter a 'channel' who seems nonchalant, isn't 'reluctant' to do so, I go in the other direction!

AND, *everything is channeled – everything!!!* We are, after all, living antennae. And we choose and cultivate the vibrations we will attune to.

One such vibration has for the history of humanity been the illusion of separation, and the reality of fear, and the choice for self-imposed limitation, lack, and the need for complexity. One could say the world is the attempt to prove there is so much to fear.

It's time for a new Game: the recovery of Oneness, and the power of Love.

## Do you experience an enlightened state? All the time? Most of the time? Some of the time?

I live perpetually in enlightenment, if that means constant awareness of the True Self. This means I know nothing, and must be fully in reliance upon God. It does *not* mean everything goes 'my' way! (That is why most folks want enlightenment: they hope it will fulfill the ego-self. It doesn't; it destroys it!) I get hungry, cry, laugh, and need extra sleep at times. So what? But I do not resist any aspect of human life whatsoever. It 'shimmers' for me: Oneness shines constantly in the dance of the Many. And, to my amazement, God works through me despite my humanity! Now, that is cause for Praise!

## What would you most want to share with the world?

That it is really is safe to let go the grip of fear, and of 'self.' It is okay to love for no good reason. It's safe to quit that job you really hate, and to begin living instead of surviving. Its okay to take a stand for heaven on earth, and work your fingers to the bone to feed hungry children, if that is the calling in your heart. And its equally okay to make love all day, and eat copious amounts of chocolate! Its okay to be radically free and awake, and its okay to give up 'G.O.O.' – Good Opinions of Others. As St Augustine once said: "Love God, and do whatever you will."

> ~
>
> *Just love the Beloved One. Let Her stream carry you. Give freedom to all beings, and encourage them to spread their wings and fly.*
>
> ~

Just love the Beloved One, and let Her stream carry you. Give freedom to all beings, and encourage them to spread their wings and fly.

Want nothing from anyone – except to ask them to remember you in their prayers when they pause from their flying, flying ever more deeply into the radiant depth of the Presence of God.

Go ahead. Die into this Divine Fire. Become the Enlightened One. Be Radical Freedom. The world suffers while it waits, for you, O sweet Messiah!

For, in the end, you must realize a life not lived for your self, because there isn't one. Rather, become utterly surrendered into That One.

Only Fear can separate you from the Love God IS.

This is the only thing you must resolve, and the only purpose the world has for anyone. And the world will go on for you just as it has, until this Mystery is resolved. Then, you will be free in the midst of it. No one will understand you. You will have no safety, no possessions, no certainty.

But you will have finally discovered what you once gave away: freedom, Reality, and God. And all 'things' will have been made new.

*What would you most want to share with the world?*

# Stepping Stones #2

When you next find yourself alone, perhaps feeling just a little lonely and the mind is spinning with thoughts and you are feeling just a little weak and out of sorts – pick up a telephone book, take three deep breaths, and with each breath say to yourself,

"In reality I remain as I am created to be. I am the holy child God."

Then merely open the phone book. Place your hand on one of the pages with the many names and numbers and just feel your way to a specific name and number (and you'll know the feeling) and then, for the fun of it, call that person. And when they answer the phone say,

"I am not here to sell you anything. I just need fifteen seconds of your time. I know that you have never met me, but I was sitting in my chair remembering that the truth is true always. And I am calling to remind you that you are loved by God. You have never failed. You have never done anything wrong. You remain pure and innocent, even now. And I wanted to give my blessings to you. Have a nice day. Goodbye."

*Source (20)*

The realm of possibilities is as infinite as you are. And the ones you select and choose are the ones that will create the web of relationships that you will call your life.
*Source (21)*

You have come forth from That which, alone, is eternally real. And because you have come forth from It, you are One with It, always.
*Source (22)*

Grace does not descend until your Father knows that you are willing to prepare a place to receive it.
*Source (23)*

Father, what would you have me do this day? How might I be of service as your plan for the Atonement is achieved in human consciousness?
*Source (24)*

The events that you experience are always neutral. And what you see occurring in the world around you remains neutral until *you* make the decision what it will be – *for you.*
*Source (26)*

Far too many seek to assist others when all it does is truly oppress them.
*Source (25)*

What if you were
to decide to create
a self that sees
itself as perfectly
unlimited?

## Chapter 5

# Birth and Life:

## The mysteries of incarnation

Where there is no conscious awareness, there can be no enlightenment, period. Only as the soul makes aware its entire journey, *from pre-conception*, through womb and birth, and on to its current place, can it ever hope to have any chance to fully awaken in a genuine liberation.

Awakening in its truest essence requires a journey of becoming fully aware of the soul itself, of its entire journey. Without this, there simply is no Core Release of the one thing from which has sprung the ego/false self: fear. Fear emerges from, and is fueled by, what is unconscious.

Fear of what we don't really know about ourselves (or are too afraid to discover) creates resistance to change, growth, healing, and even of genuine spiritual unfolding. Frankly, all of our suffering can be traced to one thing: resistance to the process whereby awareness, healing, and understanding are birthed. Every plant grows according to the quality of the seed and the conditions in which it is planted. This is no less true for the incarnation of the soul. To turn attention inward, to discover what rests in our pre-conscious memory banks, held in the very tissue and cells of our bodies, to understand that we can access and know everything about the conditions in which we first came to "land" on this planet, is not only amazing, it is liberating!

★★★★★

~

*As I opened up the Pandora's Box of emotion, I re-lived, vividly, everything that had happened that day forty-nine years ago, the day I was birthed in emergency caesarean, my mother nearly dying, my father racing through the tiny hospital of a rural town in Iowa, U.S.A., as the dead body of my twin brother was taken from the womb we had shared blissfully for eight months and twenty-seven days. He had been dead for the past three days.*

~

I dug my hands into the soil, tears streaming, body quaking in anguish, deep guttural groans and cries flowing in an endless stream. Suddenly images of my identical twin's tiny and crumbling bones, there inside the buried casket, came to view. With it I heard his 'voice':

*"They discarded me here, and a part of me has been trapped here, waiting to be recognized, to be loved, to be set free. Help set me free!"*

I opened up my body deeply with breath, breaking through the tightness gripping at my belly, my heart, my hips, my jaw. As I opened up the Pandora's Box of emotion, I re-lived, vividly, everything that had happened that day forty-nine years ago, the day I was birthed in emergency caesarean, my mother nearly dying, my father racing through the tiny hospital of a rural town in Iowa, U.S.A., as the dead body of my twin brother was taken from the womb we had shared blissfully for eight months and twenty-seven days. He had been dead for the past the three days.

I saw and felt my mother's withdrawal into shame and depression, believing surely God had 'punished' her through this for something she could not understand. I felt my brother's anguish at being discarded there; a tombstone had not been erected for four months after his burial, and no one ever visited the grave. He was never talked about, except in casual passing. That day, I felt the remnants of his soul set free.

*More importantly, a new level of wholeness emerged in me.* It was not merely an intellectual understanding, but a viscerally felt wholeness born of deep insight into the 'soil' of emotional shock, and suddenly so very much of my own recurring life challenges made perfectly good sense.

For three days, I visited the grave, offering myself up to whatever needed to be felt, remembered, and healed. Although I had done deep re-birth work before, only now were the deepest roots of this experience melted into light. And with them went a huge piece of gripped fear/resistance that nothing had released until those three days. Then, I remembered Jeshua's words:

*You cannot transcend*

*what you have not embraced with love.*

I also realized that, for all of us, what is left unembraced will call us and call us and call us, until we do embrace it. In fact it will "hold" us until we do. How does it call us? Through our nagging discomforts. Through our health problems that keep recurring. Through our failed relationships. Through our inner sense of incompletion. How can there be wholeness when a part of our own journey is yet fragmented from our consciousness?

Following this breakthrough, it was relatively easy to flow back through the womb experience, and eventually into the roots of how I, as soul, set all this up — and why. As I finally broke through, and became conscious of my *pre-conception* state, why I chose these particular parents and time frame, and the deep and personal purposes of the soul itself. As the mystic poet Rumi says:

*The mind has its reasons for everything.*

*But the soul? The soul is here for its own purposes.*

Amen to that! So very much more occurred during that period, and after, but it is not important for you. What is important is what I said a moment ago: *a new level of wholeness emerged in me.* I have learned deeply in my spiritual journey of some thirty years, that we do not awaken by acquiring new ideas and beliefs, and gathering metaphysical data. Truth emerges in the process of making the unconscious conscious, by embracing what has been fragmented, by discovering the power of Love to unite our very own being wholly, irrevocably, in the shimmering Light of Awareness. As Carl Jung put it:

*We do not awaken by imagining beings of Light.*

*But by making the darkness light.*

The complete journey of self-awareness IS the process of genuine spiritual awakening.

★★★★★

Here are a few questions you may never have pondered:

• What was going on for my mother during the time she carried me? (Mom's psyche is the "soup" in which we simmer for nine months! It takes one-sixteenth of a second for strong emotion in mom to flood the fetus.)

• How did my conception occur? (You actually carry that knowledge within you. Was love really present?)

• When my parents discovered they were pregnant with me, was the response joy or fear/sadness/anger? Did it result in closeness or distance? (Ever felt a nagging, underlying sense of not really being wanted?)

> ~
>
> *Awareness is 90% of real healing and change! From there, it is simple to begin asking: "How do I want it to be now?"*
>
> ~

• What did I begin to learn in the womb about nurturance, support, and safety?

• Was I born on time? Were drugs used? Intervention (forceps, surgery, etc)?

• Was my mother present for me right after birth? Did I bond with her and receive nurturance at her nipple in this shocking new world?

• What dynamics were at play between my mother and my father? (Our first lessons in male-female energies, relational safety, and love or the lack of it.)

You might be surprised if you take just fifteen minutes, relax the body and mind, and simply witness what emerges as you gently ask a few of these questions.

All of these questions point toward dynamics that play a huge role in creating the foundation of our psychology, and subsequent personality development. With hundreds of people I have worked with, it has been a joy to see the "light come on" as they discover these underlying dynamics, and the effects they created throughout their lives. Awareness is 90% of real healing and change! From there, it is simple to begin asking: "How do I want it to be now?"

Why is understanding the soil of our psychological development important? Not simply because it affords us the opportunity to become liberated from unconscious patterns, *but because these patterns are insights into the soul's purposes for this life*: what energies it chose to take on and transmute, what it wanted to learn, and so on.

This is so very, very important:

The soul chooses incarnation. At no time are any of us a victim of circumstance. The soul will incarnate either as a result of unhealed patterns from the past, and *thus re-create the same effects so that the opportunity for healing can occur,* OR it will do so deliberately from full consciousness, *out of its compassion and love, literally entering human life to transmute and heal patterns that have afflicted that family stream of beings for generations.*

As we become conscious of our unique incarnations, we discover these deep jewels of wisdom concerning the soul's real intent for this life, and are liberated from the nagging sense — felt and held bodily — that there has been something 'wrong' with us, or perhaps karma really exists, etc.

We become not only increasingly empowered from our real center (as opposed to mere egoic will and affirmation and drives), *we begin to increasingly fall in love with ourselves as soul, discovering within us a reservoir of infinite strength, compassion, wisdom, and peace.*

Why? The world only looks difficult to the degree we are still having difficulty loving our selves, our true Selves. We remain cut off from our true Selves exactly to the degree that we are unconscious about our own journey in its depths.

★★★★★

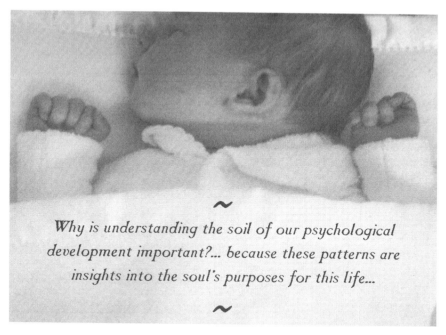

~

*Why is understanding the soil of our psychological development important?... because these patterns are insights into the soul's purposes for this life...*

~

Three basic and important things occur during the Birth Matrix:

1. Our relationship to, and capacity for, the full range of feeling and emotion is set.

2. Our core beliefs about love and support (or the lack thereof) are set.

3. Our fundamental sense of our worthiness and lovability are set.

Secondly, but equally impactful, are the following:

• How we respond to our own creativity is set (creativity, visioning, is a 'birthing' energy).

• How easily or not we 'emerge' by sharing ourselves openly with the world is set. (For example, if my birth caused painful problems for my mother, I will take on and hold a pattern of fearing the birth of my own greatness: 'my birthing causes pain.')

• How well we receive life support, and extend it, is set. (For example, a child whose body battles against mother's smoking, alcohol, and so on, tends to create a personality that doesn't easily open to trust the quality of support of the world; a child who is suddenly 'cut off' from nurturance at birth, or before, can have difficulty letting go and giving freely of time, energy, or money, for there may not be support later.)

★★★★★

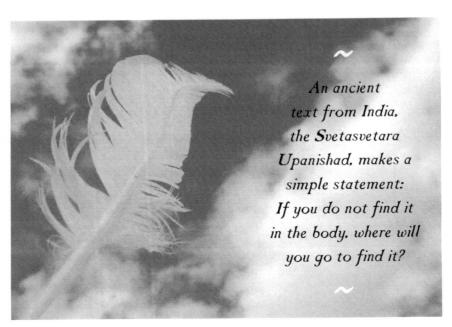

~

*An ancient text from India, the Svetasvetara Upanishad, makes a simple statement: If you do not find it in the body, where will you go to find it?*

~

Einstein once said that the only question we need answer is: "Is the universe a safe place, or not?"

This sense of safety begins at conception, and is profoundly determined before actual birth. Even if life after birth is traumatic, there may be in the memory a sense of what safety and love and life can be like. This can fuel the drive for us to heal our woundedness, or to make a better life. It is in our memory.

An ancient text from India, the Svetasvetara Upanishad, makes a simple statement:

"If you do not find it in the body, where will you go to find it?"

One thing has become clear to me over the past thirty years dedicated zealously to the process of enlightenment:

*What all beings want is to experience*
*fullness, peace, and wholeness,*
*Right here, in space-time, right now,*
*as a living, breathing being.*

The Buddha said that even the gods and goddesses envy those of us incarnate in this world as physical beings, for only here may we truly work out our salvation.

I have learned that no soul will rest until it has discovered how to be fully incarnate in its innate wholeness, right here in this pile of flesh. You see, this is what we came here for.

There is no bypass of the genuine spiritual journey, which is the journey into embodied wholeness. Yet bypass fills most of the New Age, and virtually all forms of religious systems. And the world mind? Bypass is its constant mantra!

Eventually, each and every soul must answer the call to turn around and within and discover all that has been fragmented, so that it can be consciously embraced and brought "home" in Love. This is when the "Second Birth" – the mystical birthing of Christ Mind or Buddha Mind – can truly flower.

When the darkness (what has been rendered unconscious and fragmented) is embraced whole bodily, light pours in. The dove of peace descends and does not depart, regardless of conditions. The 'hungry ghost' within is quelled, and dissolves like mist before the sun. Then, Life begins – the true life every mystic and master has raved about and called us to.

Embracing our own Birth Matrix is a tremendous piece of the puzzle of lasting peace. I encourage you to explore it.

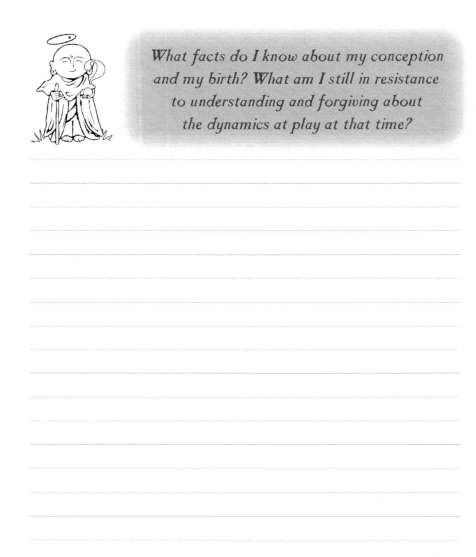

*What facts do I know about my conception and my birth? What am I still in resistance to understanding and forgiving about the dynamics at play at that time?*

How, then, does an Awakened One live? I gave you the answer earlier:
any way that the Awakened One wants to! And here now, please understand,
we come to the essence of what we'll be doing this year. For no longer will we
live in questions about what we ought to do. No longer will I ask you to live in
questions of what went wrong, but rather, in the purity of the power of the one
question that God dwells in constantly:

WHAT DO I WANT?

For here, in perfect surrender, is the mind returned to pure desire –
not the desire to gain for a separate self, but that which expresses the totality of
God. "What do I want?" is the question that God asks Himself as you.

Yes, it does mean you are perfectly free to enjoy the field of desire.
Are you capable of knowing what you truly want? Absolutely, once you decide
that you are not what you once believed you were. This requires only the decision
to recognise that nothing can exist save God, and that, therefore, you are That
One. You are whole and free – NOW!

I have often hinted to you that the totality of my life was my journey back to God.
I chose it freely, not because I was separate from God,
but because I had already awakened to the Truth that,

What could possibly exist except the Love of God?

And I chose, then, to look upon the body-mind and live only in the question,
What do I want?

Once again, one question that I would ask you to live
until you have fully realized your answer:

BELOVED FRIEND, OH HOLY ONE, WHAT DO YOU WANT?

And is that wanting generated by the freedom of Love or by the ridiculous
creation of a useless fear? Want only from freedom, and you will have your desire.

Source (27)

# A MEDITATION:

# LovesBreath

## *Let the eyes of the body close...*

**"Do not ask God to come to fill you.
Ask that you be the channel through
which God can enlighten the world."**

*Breath – the living bridge of the Holy Spirit (shem)
uniting Spirit and Matter, Creator and Creation,
the Beloved One and... YOU!*

*Take this moment... Turn attention willingly and gladly
toward the miracle of your pure presence, right where you
are, as you are. Notice the astounding miracle that you are
reading these words... But how? How can this be?
How can any thing, BE?*

*LovesBreath... simple witnessing of the mystery of breath
as it enters the body...fully felt in its sweetest, simplest
aspect...attention descending down into the belly, ahhh...*

*Five minutes in this way... only LovesBreath... resting into
pure presence... breath... feeling... sounds...*

*Open your eyes as you rest in LovesBreath.
Let it remain your primary field of awareness, even as you
become aware of images created by the play of light
through your eyes: the things around you.*

*Let the Breath become deeper, fuller, slower,*
*yet very gentle, without effort.*

*Imagine golden light (or, if you do not visualize easily,*
*simply think of light) pouring into you from the crown*
*of your head with the in-breath;*
*the Light is breathing into you...*
*all the way to the heart.*

*Now... as you exhale, imagine, see, or feel this Light/energy*
*expanding outward from your heart in all directions,*
*filling and permeating all that you see, feel, and hear.*

*Imagine that your body actually exists*
*in a luminous field of subtle, sweet Light.*

*Notice the stillness at the end of each exhale.*
*Release all efforting. Just be what you are: a living channel*
*through which Light seeks to be breathed into Creation...*
*just another five minutes, in this way.*

*God bless you...*
*God bless you...*
*God bless you...*

Source (28)

The Way of Mastery is much simpler
than you think. It rests on your
decision to use time to be wholly
committed to awakening from the
narrow constraints you have placed
upon your vast field of consciousness.

*Source (29)*

## Chapter 6

# Vitamin G

## Gratitude is the attitude of enlightenment

L et's try it on for size. Not later, as in, "When I have perfected my soul through years of spiritual penance." Not later, as in, "As soon as I solve this problem with my mate/finances/children." Not later, as in, "As soon as I am done being angry." Not later, but right now.

### RULE ONE:

*There is no 'later' in enlightenment,*
*because there is only the Eternal Now, always.*

Just as one cannot whistle and chew crackers at the same time, one cannot be in Love and fear at the same time. In Love, we are at rest in Reality. In fear, we are restless in dreams (even if our eyes are open). Only in Love can enlightenment flower, and only in Love can we discover that gratitude is the attitude of enlightenment.

## RULE TWO:

### Only Love is Real. If, in any moment, we are not in Love, we are not anywhere at all.

So, here we go: Just now, only be fully present. Presence in your awareness only what actually, is. Where are you as you read these words. State it out loud. What time is it? (Hint: it is always, now.) What do you actually feel? (Hint: thoughts are not feelings/sensations.) Presence the body: what do you notice? State it out loud.

Webster's dictionary defines gratitude as "feeling or showing that one values a kindness received."

Please read that definition at least three or four times, slowly, and contemplate the meaning of its key words: *feeling, showing, values, kindness, received.*

You see, gratitude is an attitude that must absolutely come to involve your entire being: the apprehension of the intellect, the preserving without resistance of the awareness of the object, person, place, thing, or insight, the feeling state throughout the entire body of receiving kindness, and – above all – the movement in one's entire being that kindness has been received.

Let's return to the start of our exercise, above. Okay? You know where you actually are in this moment, what time it is, and what you feel in the body.

## RULE THREE:

### Existence is a Mystery that no one has ever comprehended, or ever will. No one. It is given. Have you ever really, truly, accepted and received it?

Right now, you are experiencing the given gift of Presence. Pure awareness of the Now Moment. You don't really know how one atom of any of it has arisen! You are abiding in a tremendous, all-encompassing Mystery forever beyond any hope of comprehension, and you are most certainly not the One who brought it all into existence (contrary to the many shallow-minded and self-styled gurus of the New Age). You know through your choice to fully presence this Now Moment that you exist as pure awareness. But *how* you exist as pure awareness turns to mush any mind that sincerely inquires into it!

So, let's take the next step. Simply, out loud and slowly, repeat the following three or four times, with full deliberate and whole-being presence:

"Thank you, for all that is, Now."

Follow each repetition with a deep, slow inhale and exhale.

Now, ask yourself this question:

"Do I value, really, the fact of my pure existence?"

Hint: if the answer is "no," or "maybe," or "to a degree," then you are not in Love. If you don't know what that means, refer to Rule Two!!

Take your time, and deliberately repeat the exercise until you get a whole-being "yes."

When you honestly know that you are in a true "yes," take the next step:

## RULE FOUR:

*The given fact of pure existence (the power of awareness)*
*is a kindness extended to you, and for you,*
*and for a very amazing reason.*

So, the next step is: deliberately choose to value the kindness extended. Value your direct experience of pure awareness of this Now Moment as a kindness extended to you and for you.

And go no further until you do. (I almost wrote, 'until you can,' but of course, you 'can,' in any moment you choose to. But you know that, don't you?)

And now, for the grande finale of this priceless exercise that will radically awaken and transform your life if you make use of it repeatedly (hint, hint):

## RULE FIVE:

*Enlightenment demonstrates the power,*
*reality, and value of Love's Presence in the moment,*
*as the moment, and for the moment.*

Think about it: of the myriad ways life plays itself out and onward, there is a quality that – for all beings everywhere – strikes one to the soul with the most priceless of values: it is that quality palpable in us and around us, oozing in the air; those wonderful moments when, unmistakably, Love is present, outshining and dissolving everything else in its brilliance. It is what every soul yearns for, it is what alone heals, it is the highest of the high, and the most precious of the precious – right? Really, think about it. Of all that you have experienced, what quality, truly, is found in the most utterly precious moments you have known? (Now, refer to Rule Two, and consider how many moments you have actually had in which you were abiding in Reality! Ouch!)

So, go ahead: show that you value the kindness extended to you from utter Mystery, as your very present pure existence, with some action that reveals the presence of Love, thus demonstrating that you have truly received it.

But first, re-read this critical step three or four times, slowly, because it reveals a Divine Law of spirituality, and reveals in its doing the truth with which we started: Gratitude is the attitude of enlightenment.

a) One values the kindness extended from Mystery as one's present pure existence ...

b) and takes an action revealing Love ...

c) demonstrating that the value of what is given has been received.

This fundamental Divine Law is also a cornerstone of genuine spiritual practice, and spiritual practice is really an alchemical fire that transforms the very seat of the soul itself, burning up the false self and spewing out its ashes.

## *RULE SIX:*

*You cannot get Love, you can only receive it, and you can only fully receive it, by giving it away.*

As Jeshua (Jesus) put it in *A Course in Miracles*: "To have all, give all."

So, go ahead. Complete the exercise by extending Love, right now, right where you are in your 'world,' then come abide with me, yet a little while longer.

Aaaaah, feels good, doesn't it? Now, reflect: As you took the final step of Love's extension, did you have any regrets over the past? Any worries over the future? No! Because Love only exists in Reality, and Reality is only present in the Eternal Now! You literally just lived enlightenment. Yippieeeeeee!!!

You weren't behaving to get attention, money, comfort, love, sex, food, or any other commodity with which to feed that voraciously hungry critter we all too often keep inside: Ego. And, you experienced a state of pleasurable flow because the grip of fear was absent.

This reveals, of course, that all forms of our suffering stem from a lack of flow of Love through us into the world. Each time we have suffered (doubt, depression, confusion or reluctance to make a choice, and so on) something has occurred in the field of our awareness that has successfully interrupted the flow of Love through us into the world.

And here is the secret to it all: what has occurred is that we have not deliberately chosen to turn our attention to the act of receiving it! Events in the world around us, and/or the train of thoughts arising within us, have effectively caused us to separate from receiving the given Reality of our pure existence in Mystery. Cut off from the power of true gratitude for the very gift of our pure existence, we have forgotten Reality, and replaced it with fearful dreams; we have lost Eternity and replaced it with the ravages of Time (regrets of the past, worries of the future); we have lost Reality, and gone, where?

And in this state of un-enlightenment, we cannot hope to fulfill the one purpose for which our existence has been given. Now, take this in slowly, let it sort of roll around in your being the way you would a fine wine in your mouth. Swallow it slowly, and let it digest.

## RULE SEVEN:

*Our only purpose is to bless the world through the extension of Love through our chosen actions.*

We can negate every other pseudo purpose the mind may concoct:
* we are not here to save the world
* we are not here to ensure our children's future
* we are not here to find our soulmate
* we are not here to get rich
* we are not here to fix what's broken
* we are not here to judge anything
* and, most importantly, we are not here for ourselves.

The world once received the story about us. It was told in flesh and blood two thousand years ago. We are celebrated every Christmas, did you know that? They've even made movies about us. Shhhh... some aren't ready for Truth just yet. No need to say anything at all! Just reside in gratitude, and let Love pour through us into this world. For, you see, we are the Messiah sent in Love's name, to make Love known in this dream-world.

Nothing is preventing you from the wisdom of the Messiah. Choose to apply this exercise to every Now Moment, and learn the lesson of the radically free: only Love is Real! And each and every Now Moment is but the context into which Mystery has sent you to demonstrate that nothing can limit the power of Love!

Stop waiting for your world to change; it doesn't need to! Just give the gift everyone is secretly longing for, and by so giving, receive it. Let the world (mate, children, boss, church, government, etcetera, off the ego's hook. There is no source by which to get Love, only the choice to abide in gratitude, and the action of extending Love.

And when you master applying this exercise to everything — and I do mean everything — that arises for you, you will know truly and completely: **Gratitude is the attitude of Enlightenment.**

And you will laugh without ceasing, in good times and bad, in darkness and light, in comings and goings — yes, you will laugh with the radically free.

I am alone in this small studio apartment lent to me by a friend for a few weeks. I forgot to pick up groceries, and am aware of some hunger arising in the body. It's been humid, so I am a bit sticky from sweat. Oh, God, what an orgasm this pure awareness of the moment is! I value its gift beyond all price, and my cells tingle in bliss as I open and receive this extraordinary Presence!

Thank you, for all that Is, now.

And now, the juicy part: the act of discovering a way to extend Love into the world. Hmm, I think I will sit down and let Spirit write that article and send it to *Way of the Heart Journal* to publish. As usual, I will learn something along with my brothers and sisters.

There! And the hunger is gone...

*What ten things in my life right now
am I truly grateful for?*

1.

2.

3.

4.

5.

6.

7.

8.

9.

10.

# A MEDITATION:

# Open the Shutters
# of the Heart

*Let the eyes of the body close...*

*Release the sense of rigidity from the body, and from the mind, and especially from the breath; and in this moment, in just this one moment, allow yourself to set aside what you have perceived to be your worries and concerns and troubles. In just this one moment allow yourself to set aside every perception you have ever held about anyone. In just this moment allow yourself to set aside every perception you have ever held about what the world is for...*

*Join with me in the quiet place of the heart and set there upon the altar your belief in the past, your anticipations for the future. Release the world from your mind.*

*Let the breath flow deeply and freely without need to constrict or direct it. Allow it to flow through you gently and easily... and use the power given unto you, not to make, but to allow yourself to begin to truly join with me... and if you believe that must be hard, realize that is just a perception. Set it aside, replace it with a loving thought that teaches you communion with all that Jeshua is, simple and natural... for minds that are joined cannot be separate one from the other.*

*Open then the shutters of the heart. Touch deeply the place of peace within you.... and begin to see and to feel the soft and warm and radiant light that seems to have always been there. Touch that light. Allow yourself to be bathed within it. Breathe that light....allowing every obstruction,* every obstacle to the presence of love, to be dissolved from the mind, from the emotion and from the body itself... feel me then as I come to abide with you now... for I am not limited... and yet I am no different from you, with the same unlimitedness as shared by us. And the place of peace is not lost to us... and abiding there without trace of effort, hear then these words that come not through a mind or body outside of you. But hear them as if they come from your own soul, through your mind, and touch your own lips.

"There is nothing outside of me, my radiance knows no boundary, my purity has not been tainted, my innocence remains forever and I am embraced in the love that is the presence of God. My light has no beginning and it shall not have an end and with it I embrace all things and in embracing them, I heal them and transcend them. I am the one in whom my Father remains eternally well pleased. I am the one who has come into the world, and the world has comprehended me not. I am come to bring light and to reveal it to my brothers and to my sisters, for they are not outside of me, and everyone that I behold, in them do I see and know myself. They are, then, my salvation, and because I give my love to them without measure, I receive the love of Christ... I am that one! I am that one! I have lived the life of every being and the light that is Christ lives within me."

Choosing light, I light up all darkness.
Choosing love, I release all fear,
and because I am awake in God's love
the whole of creation is uplifted in me.
Gone the perception
of the need to suffer.
Gone the perception of lack and of loss.
Gone the perception that I have ever
been separate from love.

*And because I embrace the world,*
*the world is transformed,*
*and now is my purpose before me,*
*and the truth of my being revealed.*
*I come only as a friend of everyone,*
*and because I extend my love,*
*they are healed in my presence,*
*and from this moment on I choose*
*to go out no more from*
*my Father's Holy Place.*

*And the whole body becomes but the means through which I make my love manifest to the world. I live, yet not I, but Christ lives in me. One mind, whole, complete forever. I am the peace that must pass all understanding. I am the light that lights all worlds... And because there are no boundaries even now, without moving a muscle, I allow my light to expand until it touches every heart in this one small room, for I am asked only to receive those who are sent unto me; and in receiving them I know that I am received, and my light heals the heaviness on all hearts; and embracing my brothers and sisters I remember that we are but One. Abide then in that place of union and leave it not. Be not in a hurry, for where is there to go beyond this?*

*Once we dreamt a dream and for just one moment we chose to believe we were separate, but the time of dreaming is ending now, and because I choose to awaken, my brothers and sisters can awaken within me.*

*For this am I created; for this alone am I sent forth; for this have I entered the world; for this have I suffered the world; and for this I enlighten this world. And now in this moment that is both without beginning and end, understand well that you hold the power to forgive the world, and if there is anyone or any event you have ever known that somehow* rests as a chain upon the heart go to that event, go to that experience, go to the presence of that one in your mind and embrace them with that light, and know that you are safe right now to allow miracles to heal whatever has been in the past. Choose it then, choose it well. For the reluctance to forgive has been the only thing that has ever blocked your awareness to the truth and kept it from your mind and from your heart.

Forgiveness is the great need of this world and you are the one who can bestow it... And if that feels just a little difficult, remember that you are not alone, because I am with you and I will indeed give you my strength until yours is as certain as mine. Ask it of me and it is yours. Some of you are becoming aware, in the quiet place of peace, that you are indeed never alone; for even as I am with you, there are other friends who are likewise with you. Trust what you feel and what you yourself know. Not with the mind but with the heart. Forgive, then, the world and you have forgiven yourself; and in forgiving yourself the heart begins to open. It begins to trust in safety, and peace comes to be remembered.

## Together we are the light that lights this world.

Begin now to just let the breath move a little more deeply in the body as if you were a breathing in life itself, just saying "yes" to it. It's never hidden from you at any moment. It's as though all the love of God, in soft, golden, gentle light is just pouring into the very cells of your being. And yet you do nothing but receive what is rightfully yours.

## Because you are, the love of God is made present.

*Source (30)*

Long have I waited for this age to be upon this plane, this world of yours. For soon the Son will no longer suffer the torment of the dream of separation.

*Source (31)*

## Chapter 7

# Jesus in my Living Room

## A commentary on communion with Christ offered by a reluctant channel

Okay, so I am not a *Course in Miracles* student. However, over the last nine years, I have had an opportunity to get to know its primary author fairly well.

When Jesus (he asked that I refer to him by the name by which I had known him in his last incarnation: "Jeshua") first appeared to me out of a field of brilliant light in my apartment, as I was rushing about in order to get to work, it was the incomprehensible love which embraced me in waves that caught my attention sufficiently to overcome the intense resistance and fear of my well-formulated and deeply embedded ego. Two years of daily apprenticeship filled with internal struggling – fear of going crazy, fear of being ridiculed – and many instances of miracles and personal healing would pass by before I was willing to surrender to this process and offer it to Spirit to be used in whatever way it wished to. I put up one heck of a fight!

Still, His patience, love, and great teaching skill, revealing a wisdom some part of me was thirsting for, kept carrying me deeper and deeper into Reality. As I began to make myself available for Him to communicate with others through me, I had the immediate experience of witnessing the healing occurring in hundreds of others, while the process also served to create learning contexts for me: understanding and handling projection, overcoming fear of others' opinions, recognizing how deeply invested I had been in the unconscious pattern of making others idols and substitutes for the Reality of God's Love. My deep resistance to the fulfillment of my assigned function was directly related to my belief that others' approval of me held a greater value than my own emerging awakening into union with God.

For several years I constantly demanded that He prove himself to me. I had to know it was more than just my own mind. He accommodated me with, yes, patience and love. The objective instances in which not even I (trained in critical philosophy) could explain away the validity of Jeshua as an intelligence/being independent of my "self" kept growing. Recently, after over nine years of this experience, my resistance and doubt have finally abated. I merely join with my Brother in the certainty of knowledge; in the grace of a genuinely holy relationship, for I have come to join Him in having looked within and realizing there is no lack. Out of loving gratitude and celebration, I have come to join with Him in realizing that Love does, indeed, heal. I join with Him to create only what extends our shared treasure: the reality of God's Love.

To echo Robert Perry's question in his article, 'An Editorial on Jesus Channeling' published in *On Course* in September, 1996: *What do we make of people purportedly channeling the author of* A Course in Miracles? *What do we make of this material?* These are worthwhile questions, I suppose, *but only for those who have chosen to make the* Course *a "seat of authority" in their own unique journey of awakening,* and perhaps, have a need to "resolve" a perceived

*For several years
I constantly demanded that
He prove himself to me.
I had to know it was more
than just my own mind.*

conflict, threat, or (on the other hand) make sure they aren't missing the latest Divine Revelation!

Can the communications coming from Jesus through myself, Brent Haskell, Tom Carpenter, or others (I know only of Tom and Brent, and Jeshua assured me that He was, in fact, working through and with them) be used improperly? Of course. Can the communications coming from Jesus through Helen Schucman be used improperly? Of course (or should I say, "of *Course*"?) Can they assist the willing mind and heart to release its illusions and awaken ever more deeply into Love's Presence? Of course. And just this is a point I think is worth making. I take it from what Jeshua teaches through me, over and over, to others:

> *There is nothing outside oneself with the power*
> *to awaken us, nor to deny that awakening,*
> *for the one gift of the Father to the Son*
> *is the power and freedom*
> *to choose which voice to hear:*
> *that of Love, or that of fear.*

One tendency of our minds is to make a fundamental error, the error of confusing *content* with *form*. Jeshua has shared with me that *A Course in Miracles* is but one form of a "Universal Curriculum," the aim of which is to bring about the overcoming of Separation, returning the Son to His rightful place of perfect union with the Father. Like fingers pointing at the moon, the myriad forms of this universal curriculum are not the same thing as the moon itself. In my own journey, I finally caught on to how the ego just loves to seduce me into becoming entranced with the fingers in its attempt to delay me from absorbing the light and beauty of the moon!

I would suggest that if any mind feels compelled to resolve a perceived conflict between the *Course* and other forms of the universal curriculum, even other forms of teaching which Jesus may be involved in, it may be because a subtle attachment to a beloved *form* of teaching is present. One way to discover if it is, is to do the following: if you feel caught up in this "issue" simply throw your copy of the *Course* away, and refrain from quoting it, going to *Course* groups/workshops, and so on, for at least six months. And never let yourself utter to another, "Well, the *Course* says..." (I once had to do the same with my attachment to yoga.)

I would like to end this offering with a few simple things I have gleaned from my experience as a daily student of Jesus/Jeshua:

*No one knows what their brother or sister needs.*
*Nothing has any purpose or value*
*save what the Holy Spirit gives it.*
*Jesus assumed responsibility for the Atonement,*
*and knows what He is doing.*
*Only the ego compares.*
*Only ego can fear, or feel threatened.*
*The ego loves to take responsibility for*
*"protecting" and "fixing" others.*
*The goal of any form of curriculum*
*lies beyond the form itself,*
*in an immediate Knowledge by Being,*
*not a knowledge About.*

Vigilance and the cultivation of deep self-honesty are a hallmark of every form of the universal curriculum I have ever studied (and that has been virtually all spiritual/psychological disciplines.) The very key to awakening is to make conscious the subtle and slippery ways of ego, so that they become transparent and we withdraw our value from them, choosing Love instead. This penetration of the ego-mind's mechanics is a major component of what the *Course* offers to any dedicated student. Yet, the *Course* is not an end in itself. It is a tool for re-training the mind to think with God. The goal? Once correction comes, then the journey of creation can truly begin! Just as a painter learns how to correctly use brushes and color, the corrected mind becomes a fit communication device for the extension of Love, and such extension is both endless and eternal. The ego seeks an end, a resolution. The awakened mind, being no longer in the conflict of split-mindedness caused by fear, merely "shows up" in each moment, chanting quietly one mantra: "How can I extend my treasure this day?" And what can that treasure be but the Reality that it is one with its Creator, and only Love is real?

To anyone reading this offering, please... Waste no more time comparing, contrasting, questioning whether this form is "truer" than that form of the curriculum. Waste no more time in analyzing things in order to deduce whether or not other forms are "congruent" with the Course. Love is not a logical construct. It is a decision and a commitment that transcends the way the world thinks and perceives. Debate and analysis is great for minds that want to delay stepping into the Reality of **being** *what all forms of the curriculum teach*.

Jesus has one goal: to help us into the lived realization that we are what He is, and to get on with joining Him in the Resurrection of Awakening, to let His very words become ours: *I and My Father are One.* There is no greater task, nor any greater need of courage in this world, than to give up seeking and acknowledge that we have found, for stepping into complete responsibility for all that we think, all that we do, and all that we feel. As Alan Watts so deftly put it: "Once you have received the answer, hang up the phone, and put it into action, into your very lived experience."

The great (apparent) paradox of awakening is that one truly becomes very "ordinary." That is, one simply is present in each moment with no agenda, no plan, no beliefs. The mind emptied of "self" becomes merely a conduit through which Love creates whatever may serve the Atonement, since that is the only purpose time and the body can have. Giving up the egoic need to shout "I want it my way!" and, instead, gently proclaiming, "Into Thy hands I commend my Spirit." What will follow from such surrender of illusion? Only Love can know! You might end up being a teacher of a *A Course in Miracles.* You might find yourself channeling its author! Or, perhaps you will find yourself sweeping streets...All functions, when allowed to be the conduit for Love, are equal. For the awakened, the *form* is irrelevant, the content *everything.*

> ~
>
> *Jesus has one goal: to help us into the lived realization that we are what He is, and to get on with joining Him in the Resurrection of Awakening, to let His very words become ours: I and My Father are One.*
>
> ~

Will you join with me in discovering ever more deeply the Reality of Love? Of what it can do? Of how it heals through the willing mind? Of the depth of joy that can be truly known? Of what prevents it from expressing through us? Who knows? We might even discover that we need go nowhere else to find heaven than *here*, in this (transformed) world, than *now*, in this perfectly eternal Moment...

*What am I continuing on a daily basis that no longer fulfils me?*

# The Disciple's Prayer

Father-Mother of the Cosmos,
Shimmering Light pervading All,
Ever unknowable Mystery,
Yours is the kingdom of the heart, mind and body
I once called 'mine.' To you do I return them now.

Through this heart, extend Your Presence
as Love, Compassion, Patience and Understanding.

Through this mind, express only Wisdom
to uplift, to expand, to appreciate, to nurture,
or else let it be silent.

Through this body, move only
to honour, to love, to please, to nurture,
to provide a safe embrace for anyone
who suffers and is sent to me.

Help me to remember:
It is only in giving You that I receive You,
It is only in praising You that I remember You,
And it is only in humility before You
that I may awaken to what is truly occurring
here on earth, as it is already in heaven,
and fulfill my part in Your Divine Plan.

Om, shanti, shanti, shanti, Om. Amen.

*Source (32)*

Time is not a prison for you. It is that which flows out of your very consciousness, and there is never a place or a time – never a place or a time – which is more conducive to the Way of Mastery than the place in which you are and the time that is now.

*Source (33)*

## Chapter 8

# A Call to Praying Peace

written by the very soul of the Holy City you call 'Jerusalem'

Israel Pilgrimage, 2005

The air is brisk and this ancient land that has been my home forever is thankfully quiet; no one will die this night in the latest pulse of Separation, the *intifadah* that has erupted and been sustained among my family for the past several years. A desire grows within me, and my attention draws me to the square, here in the Old City, where Palestinian, Jew, Arab, and Christian live together and care for one another. As always, my heart smiles at the sight of men and women in prayer at the Wailing Wall while — just beyond — the Temple of the Rock looms in its golden dome, while all around are the majestic spires of Christendom. It is not so hard to sense that they join with generations streaming back into time, carrying into this present moment — amidst a conflicted world — the gift born of Abraham so long ago. For here in their prayers they may touch the reality of peace, and the presence of That One who is given many names: Jehovah, Allah, Hashem, God.

This is the land in which That One revealed the truth beneath and beyond all lesser gods:

*Hear, O Israel, The Lord Thy God, is One.*

I must smile as I share what has always been my favorite phrase, reverberating through my soul like a timeless mantra. This is the land that birthed the three great world faiths of Judaism, Islam, and Christianity. Here the beautiful young man from Nazareth whose name is similar to my own, fulfilled His destiny in service to all beings. Here the young man kissed by Visions given from God, Mohammed, came in mystical flight, proclaiming this place the holiest place in Islam, second only to Mecca.

Here it is still evident that these three faiths are like strands of one thread, shaped by the march of cultures through time, yet echoing in their essence: *God is Love*. Like children occasionally stumbling or throwing a tantrum, they grow toward a maturity destined to flower and bear much good fruit for the whole world. Perhaps you think this is but the naïve faith of an elderly soul among you, but I know it is more. In time, you will, too.

On this night, the main square is dotted by Jewish boys and men in their black coats and hats, as they pass the numerous clusters of Israeli soldiers, weapons hanging from their shoulders. Beyond the wall, the golden dome of the Temple of the Rock shines in the evening lights, and I am comforted that my Arab family – though with different words – chant the songs of peace together. I always feel a *goodness* here, in this ancient and sacred place. I have always known it is the womb of the world, pregnant and waiting to birth a precious gift to the All. It is, in this land of sacred spaces, the most sacred for me.

Yet I must confess to you that my faith has sometimes faltered. It has been over two years since this latest *intifadah* began, and I have cried a tear for every needless drop of wasted blood, as brother rises up against brother, vexed by the spell that would make them see a stranger there, held in the scope of a mindless weapon. It pierces my very soul when I hear the insanity of God's holy name used to rationalise the madness of attack, and the justification of defense. This is violence, not only between brother and brother, but also against the heart of all Truth; the Truth Abraham devoted his life to revealing, and thus, violence against Creation itself. Yet, it is merely the denial of fear,

and the tragic resistance to the vulnerability and forgiveness that could heal it all in the twinkling of an eye.

It often saddens me when the media paints a picture of this land as one of eternal conflict, for it is not so. Only since the 1920s have there been deep tensions between Arabs and Jews in the Holy Land. That was when the colonial legacy of Britain in the Mid-East began, and nationalism of, first, Zionism, and then Palestinian nationalism, began and developed the "us versus them" view of what it meant to live in this land together. Things weren't perfect before then, but all the elders speak of memories of a much more harmonious time, with shared Jewish and Arab ceremonies and celebrations; weddings, births, deaths, holidays. It was once common for Islamic sheikhs to be masters of the Jewish Torah, and for rabbis to know the heart of the Qur'an and the soaring truths uttered by Islamic mystics.

The earliest of Christians shared in this rich legacy, found in Y'shua's (that beautiful young man I mentioned earlier!) true teachings that leap to life in his native language of Aramaic. For he emerged from the very soil of these first two children of Abraham, and was radical enough to take God at His word, allowing himself to be transformed into the Living Word itself. I am sure he has made Abraham proud!

I have watched this long-standing sickness reach to new heights of insanity, permeating governments world-wide, and know the world stands at the brink of a choice-point, pregnant with meaning. Like a wave rising to a crescendo, like two paths diverging from a common point, there has never been a moment of history so crucial in the battle of Light and Dark, for the hearts of mankind, and authority over the earth. You would think by now I would know that it is always at such moments of doubt that our wondrous God will grace me with a demonstration that His Plan is always at work, like the songbird who sings while dawn is yet night. This night has become such a moment. It is the moment I first see them.

★★★★★

The first thing I noticed was the familiar face of a young American–Israeli Jew, Eliyahu. His presence always reminds me that there are those steadfast in the reality of peace. I first met him when he began a weekly prayer vigil after the start of this *intifadah*. That day, he gathered with friends to chant the prayers and words of peace of both Arab and Jew. Many gravitated to their circle. When violence broke out, the soldiers made everyone leave, except Eliyahu and his friends. Even the memory comforts me now.

On this evening of *Shabat*, Eliyahu meets a group of some fifty beings – Australians, Americans, English, Dutch, German, and more. As they form a circle in the middle of the square, it is clear to me that something quite special is occurring. So quickly does this group drop into Praise-filled Presence – love glittering through their eyes – that I cannot help but call them a Family of the Heart, and instantly they are dear to me.

Who could not notice their smiles? And I confess I delighted immediately in what I can only describe as an attractive joy and aliveness. I was struck with the thought that they have come to feed this womb of the world as much as to be fed by it. In time, I would come to know just how true this was.

I cannot help but move closer to them. Even the young Hasidic Jews and elderly men are attracted, and with many, I move quietly and unobtrusively to the wall. They let their tears flow without shame, and many seem to breathe into those tears, hands and forehead against these ancient stones, and I am attracted to them all the more. Without anyone saying a word, and without formal introductions, I slip into their number, like a bee attracted to the sweet nectar of honey. I am a part of them, and it is enough they are here. Lord knows, I have had a very long life. Time enough to learn trust in the Law of the heart's attraction! I know only that these are brothers and sisters, and I shall journey with them a while.

★★★★★

During their next several days, I watched with them as they prayed, meditated, laughed, cried, and easily embraced the holy places and sheikhs of Islam, the rabbis of Judaism, and the surprising and palpable presence of Christ – certainly one of my favorite Jewish peace activists! – like an unseen breeze calling humanity to a Higher Love.

I journeyed with them to Galilee, and there marveled to realize a very old friend I had known so long ago was among them. I recall he was rather close to that beautiful young man from Nazareth. It was good to be in this fertile place along the Sea of Galilee, and memories waft through: images of Y'shua gathered with his friends to share his growing insights into what he referred to as '*malkutha,*' the queendom of heaven on earth.

I was touched by the way they opened their hearts to one another, chanting and singing and praising God, even as old wounds were cracked open, and the weight of illusions shed in rivulets of flowing emotions, holding one another with glad hearts.

I marveled with them at the Jordan River, where – together in such presence and support – they lived the ancient custom of baptism in holy waters. And I watched quietly apart from them as the waters carried away the weight of past wounds, past guilt, and celebrated with them as the past was truly passed away!

I watched how they moved through their days, and saw the impact in the faces of everyone they met from the shop owners gifted with their purchases, to those who served them in restaurants, and even their impact in the lives of their Arab tour guides.

This group was different than many of the others. They had not come as tourists to see this land. They had come to bless it, and to be blessed by the energies I, too, have sought for so long to help hold and maintain. And that made my heart soar in praise to God, as I felt my faith not only restored, but expanded in ways that surprised me!

As I journeyed with them, I learned of astounding things. Some things new to me, and things ancient which were a joy to witness being made alive again. They were determined to demonstrate the possibility of peace, by fully understanding the teaching of all religions as a call to be the presence of peace itself. Not later, when conditions change, but now!

They spoke of this new idea of *Praying Peace*, rather than praying *for* peace. I hadn't considered it before: praying *for* peace requires a judgment and fear that peace is not, and cannot be, present. It puts if off into the future!

"Precisely the problem all these centuries," I thought to myself.

They talked together and with their friends about the *extraordinary pleasure of praying a living peace.* And that is what quickened my soul from its despair. This group of pilgrims understood the heart of all the ancient teachings that have arisen in this land: the miracle of peace is discovered by choosing to *be* the presence of enjoyable peace, Now.

Every prophet has said the same, has shown the invisible doorway. But now, I began to sense a new hope. The world is now connected in ways none of the prophets could enjoy. Their message was always so limited to small bands of followers, or encrypted in texts not able to reach all hearts and minds.

I learned they had come with a Plan Not Their Own, but in response to a deep inner call of the soul. I became excited to realize they were connected to a network of beings the world over who were also joining them in specific meditations and prayers, at certain times, resting in the knowledge that because all minds are joined, and that the world is only the result of the dominant matrix held in the One Mind, they held the power to participate in the healing of world through the demonstrated renewing of their One Mind.

It was this that called them to be here, yet joined with many others all over the globe.

★★★★★

This was when I learned that the world has changed. Scientists can now measure the effects of such gatherings, and what their measurements revealed surprised even them! Richard Benishal, who uses a Biometer to measure the presence of light in meditation groups, shared that a typical reading might be in the range of 2500–3500 angstroms. But where a group comes together with such pure resonance, fueled by the Passionate Desire to be the Living Peace, he has been astounded to see readings in excess of 9600! No doubt,

*The level of Light that one group can infuse into this world can be limited only by the vision and thought held in the minds of its members.*

And inspired as this group was by the vision given them by Y'shua, limits don't stand much of a chance.

For the first time, I am feeling a new kind of hope. Not one based on the call of religion alone, but hope born of actual indications that the power of consciousness, focused through individuals joining as one, contains all the power necessary to establish the age of Light not merely in the hearts and minds of a small handful of contemplatives and mystics, but throughout the world: the coming of heaven to earth can be a reality!

This is what I have waited for. This is what I have suffered for. The time when the world can be awakened to the simple power of consciousness, when it rests in the memory of the presence of God, not passively, but in ecstatic outpouring! For all God has created creation for, is to be radiant conduits extending and growing the Queendom of heaven on earth by giving away without ceasing the unbounded Love that God IS!

> ~
>
> *For the first time, I am feeling a new kind of hope.*
>
> *Not one based on the call of religion alone, but hope born of actual indications...*
>
> ~

I have always known this love. It is what has kept me in this land for such a long, long, time. Waiting. Praying. Supporting Muslim, Arab, Jew, and Christian alike, though often unseen and underappreciated! And now, there is hope.

This simple group was part of the tip of an arrow hundreds of thousands strong, with growing numbers of feathers to keep its aim true and strong! May God inspire them to continue this Great Work, and may their numbers grow into the millions – millions of brothers and sisters who know the power of Love to heal all things, the strength of forgiveness to release all past pains, and the presence of kindness to melt all hearts, that all may discover: God IS.

Then this land will fulfill its role as the land of milk and honey, indeed! And its nourishment will pour out over the earth, feeding all of mankind with healing presence, and the birthing of the world our Creator envisions.

After all, like you, I have always known that only God's Plan can work in the end. Darkness, like a stone worn smooth by flowing waters, stands not a chance!

And so I write to say thank you, dear pilgrims. It was a joy and a blessing to be inspired by you and your courage, and I anxiously await your coming

return in September. And I write to call all brothers and sisters from all lands and spiritual walks, who know *only the Truth can be true*. Come all! Come and pray with us in the *Heart of the Christos* – that silent center where all souls are joined – until no one is left outside, unloved. May the world realize the power of Praying Peace!

I will remain faithfully yours, for I AM:
**Yerusha–Shalom**, (the manifestation of peace),
the very soul of the Holy City you call 'Jerusalem.'

*I have always known this love. It is what has kept me in this land for such a long, long, time. Waiting. Praying. Supporting Muslim, Arab, Jew, and Christian alike, though often unseen and underappreciated! And now, there is hope.*

*Is my commitment to Love or is my commitment to fear? Where in my life am I letting fear rule me?*

## 1. Desire

Are you willing to feel it and let that **thread of desire** carry you home? Can you remember to use time constructively, by focusing your intention, by reminding yourself of what you're truly here for? You're not here to survive, you're here to **live** as the Truth of who you are.

## 2. Intention

...means to utilise time each day to focus your attention on the **desire** to be Christ Incarnate. Intention is that energy, or that use of the mind, that creates (through consistent practice) the channel, if you will, through which desire begins to move down and re-educate the emotional body, and even the cellular structure of the physical body, and all of the lesser avenues of thinking that occur within the intellect – so that everything involved in your being is integrated, working together, and focused on the fulfillment of that one **grand desire** to accept your function in this world. And your function is healing your sense of separation from God.

## 3. Allowance

...not a passive acceptance of things as they are, but a recognition that there is something quite beautiful at work. There is an Intelligence, a Love that knows you better than you know yourself, and is presenting you, moment to moment, with jewels and gems and lessons and blessings – that something is weaving the tapestry of your life, and nothing is happening by accident.

## 4. Surrender

*...is the cultivation of the recognition that your happiness can be found only in the submission of your will to the Will of God. For your will has been to be in conflict and struggle and limitation. The Father's Will is that you live without conflict, in peace, and joy, and fulfillment, and happiness. It is called bliss.*

## Meditate on Humility

*Genuine humility flows from the deep-seated recognition that you cannot save yourself, that you are created and not Creator, that you are effect and not cause (in an absolute sense), that something called Life is not yours, that there is **something** beyond your capacity of containment and intellectual understanding. And if that something ever decided to give up loving you [snaps fingers], you would cease to be, that no matter how deep you go into the depth of God, and no matter how deep you achieve an awareness and consciousness of union with God, that what God is, is forever beyond your growing capacity to understand God. It is like an Ocean of Infinite Depth. And when you realize that, strive as you might, you'll never wrap your self, your little self, around that Source, you will rest into humility – g**enuine humility**.*

*Source (34)*

You are only here to be truly helpful.
Yet you do not know what needs to be done.
Would you know your Father's will for you?
Precious friends, open the eyes to your Self;
it will not be hidden from you.

*Source (35)*

# Chapter 9

# Passion & Compulsion

***What's*** *your passion? What's **your** passion?*
*What's your **passion?***

When we speak of passion, we intrinsically mean what attracts our attention so fully and deeply that we feel excitement in our cells, a warmth and expansion of the heart we conceive as love, and a burst of mental imagery and vision. Whether one's passion is Balinese gamelan music, art, football, or chocolate – or even spirituality – passion always contains these effects and qualities.

*What are you **compelled** by? What **compels** you?*
*What are your **compulsions?***

When we speak of compulsion, we intrinsically mean what moves us into action, what pushes us. We may feel as though we are pulled, as though choicelessly magnetized toward a belief, an object, an action. (Strangely, chocolate is on this list for me, too!)

Have you ever been on the phone and said to a friend, "Listen, I gotta run. I have to be somewhere in an hour." Compelled, out the door you go!

Now, imagine the same scene, except that your passion for classical music is present, there is a symphony tonight, and its time to go: "Listen, I'd love to chat, but I am just off to the symphony!"

Can you feel the difference in your body? Go ahead, stop reading on, and play with those two scenes until you notice their energies.

Now, which one did you enjoy? Which one increased a feeling of joy and aliveness? Which one felt, shall we say, freer for you?

I never cease to marvel at the enlightenment revealed on folks' faces, or how their bodies relax when they do this little experiment. Perhaps for the first time, they tap into a conscious knowing of the very real differences between passion and compulsion, for they literally feel different in the body and, thus, anyone can learn how better to know which is truly operating in their lives at any moment.

And then I ask them to think about the percentage of activities they engage in for each in a given day: Ugh! The smile goes, the shoulders drop. Compulsion, it seems, tends to outscore passion more than three to one!

★★★★★

One fundamental transformational practice is to mindfully, consciously and deliberately re-train the mind to recognise the distinction between passion and compulsion, and then gradually reduce the compulsion side of the ledger. Initially, it can be quite a shock to even entertain that it is possible to cultivate a life more and more moved by the forces of passion. Not only possible, but permissible! Here is a key teaching principle to help you:

*I need do nothing. I need not succeed,*
*I need not love or be loved, I need not live at all.*
*Since I live, I am free to let joy be my compass,*
*And my joy is measured by my passion.*

We could say it is an integral part of the spiritual awakening process to be thoroughly compelled to live our passion. *A Course in Miracles* refers to the attainment of this stage as the 'Happy Dream.' I refer to it as 'The Seamless Life,' where one's life is no longer compartmentalized: career life to satisfy the compulsion for material survival and comfort, relationship for sex and companionship, church or some such endeavor for spiritual connection, recreation to balance out work, and so on. Rather, one's work (providing material existence needs) is one's play – is one's service – is one's spiritual practice – is one's love life. In the Seamless Life, through deliberate cultivation of the art of leading with your true passion (or, being led by Passion), the usual hierarchy is reversed: we do not do to survive so that we might (hopefully) get a chance to explore our inner self or take that dream vacation or find that special love, but the Love flowing through us reveals every moment as a vacation which unfolds our inner selves, and quite effortlessly provides our material survival and reveals life itself as our lover.

Can you imagine a life in which you 'became again as a little child to enter the kingdom,' and freely trusted your passion to lead you along the way, with 'no thought for tomorrow, what you shall wear, or what you shall eat?' Here is a great Wonder Question exercise to try out:

*If I fully lived from passion, what are three things I would immediately change in my life? How would I feel right now if those changes were already in place?*

Go ahead, the soul is just a kid in an infinite candy store (some of which can make you sick)... take a few moments and abide in the questions, breathe, and allow yourself to feel and notice what comes up for you.

*For here is a critical importance between passion and compulsion: Passion can only flow in an environment of radical trust in God and in self, for passion lived is the expression of their Union.*

Whenever trust is absent there is a 'broken' heart (often cleverly disguised or simply dismissed as unimportant): that energy you felt earlier as you tuned into passion is not allowed to flow.

*And where passion is not flowing, compulsion comes to make a home. For, you see, compulsion is an energy linked to a **fear of not surviving** – and it is absolutely* imperative to get deeply that survival (no matter how apparently comfortable, healthy, rich, or stable) is not equal to living! For true life is of the soul, while only the body consciousness seeks its survival. As the great Sufi mystic, Rumi, puts it: "The mind has its reasons for everything, but the soul? The soul is here for its own purposes."

And one of the fundamental stages of the spiritual odyssey is to cultivate a life *lead by the passions of the soul.* Here, life is lived 'at the edge.' Of what? The unknown, for passion loves what is not yet known, even if it is in discovering a better chocolate!

For passion will always lead to the contexts, relationships, places, books, teachings, and teachers through which the God Who Shimmers and birthed us in Love works without ceasing and in perfect knowledge of just how to awaken the dreaming child from its nightmares, and return it to perfect peace, quiet joy, and the rest of Radical Freedom.

*And when your passion is solely to know God, you will be carried away, carried away eternally, borne on the wings of a Mystery, the taste of which is sweet above honey, until suddenly the whole of creation is transfigured, revealing the Beloved Divine smiling everywhere and as all things.*

Then fear is vanquished. The mind is stilled (not simply quieted). 'You' have disappeared, though the body plays out its final round. And in your place quietly slips the Christ, who – disguised well as just another human being – comes to bless the world, and through the movement of Love through him or her, all beings are returned to heaven; the remembrance dawns, and does not depart, that only Love has been real all the time, here in this mysterious field, where we arise and pass away, the effect of God's own happy dream.

Does discerning passion from compulsion hold importance? Are there depths to discover in one's passion? Can the divine life be known? Hey, mate, weren't you listening?

Come to the edge and lean into the unknown. Rekindle your trust, and let the heart be healed of fear: only illusions to lose, only Life to be regained. Be re-made in this golden nectar pouring from God's pitcher into His chosen cup: **you**! For God IS the passion longing to flow upward, outward, and through the heart of the beautiful, innocent, free, and loved child that you eternally shall be. As Shakespeare knew: 'the play's the thing.' Get on with the show!

*jayem*

# The Way of the Servant

*I have said before that the world is but a symbol. Choose wisely
what your world will symbolise for you, for it is the symbols you
choose which your sister will see. Thus is your heart revealed,
and you have "spoken" your judgment of the Father.*

*She who knows me walks with me, and she who walks with me
makes straight her path, and all things are given to the praise
of what God is: Love. Love embraces all things, heals all things,
transforms all things, celebrates all things, and, above all, mirrors
what God is in all things.*

*Give no thought, then, for tomorrow, neither for the things you
shall eat, nor for the things you shall wear, for the Father knows you
have need of these things, and He will not leave you comfortless.*

*When I once asked you to "take no thought" you unwittingly failed
to hear me, deciding you can direct the choice of what you
would eat, and what you would wear, and thus cleverly cherish
the "loves" you would desire to keep.*

*To decide for yourself is precisely to take thought. That is, because
you failed to let the Comforter choose for you, right-mindedness
was cast aside, and the real world abandoned. But she who praises
God in all things keeps no decision for herself, listening only to the
Voice for God, and the servant knows the Voice speaks only with
perfect reason. To cling to but one "love" you have mis-created is
surely to be unreasonable, for you have learned that the symbols of
the world can be but the symbols of death.*

*Death is no longer your will, but Life.*

*I am come again unto you that you might have Life,
and this more abundantly.*

*Learn well, then, to ask before each choice:
"Does this value the symbols of death or of Life?"*

*Abiding in innocent honesty, you will realize that the Comforter's
guidance is immediate, and uncompromising. Herein will be revealed
to you the final meaning of my teaching: Take no thought,
for the Father knows you have need of these things.*

*Source (36)*

Photography by Michael Flatt

*What is your passion?*
*What are your compulsions?*

'Surrender' means to settle into the position of the
servant, the conduit through which the Mind of
God, the Love of God, can be expressed. The mind
that exists in perfect surrender sees absolutely no
purpose to any moment of experience save this.
The mind in perfect surrender looks out upon
a world that has been healed from its own
misperception that the world has had power over it.
It sees that at no time has it experienced anything
but its own outpicturing. This is why all events are
neutral. It is mind that interprets an event, draws a
conclusion, and then bases behavior upon it.

The mind that is healed, and that rests in surrender,
looks out upon an innocent world that has been
touched by its blessing of forgiveness. And that
forgiveness is simply a step in which that mind
recognizes that the world it had thought was there
was nothing more than its own mental creation,
and smiles and laughs and sees that the world
has held no power, and that all events that have
arisen, all interpretation of events, have been
generated from within the kingdom of the mind
– the one place that it is given unto you to assume
responsibility for, as your domain.

*Source (37)*

Sexuality is God – pure and simple. Holiness occurs
when any two beings look within themselves; that is, they
make the journey within and discover the Truth that
there is no lack. Then they join, not to get,
but to create the good, the holy, and the beautiful.

*Source (38)*

# Chapter 10

# The Spirit of Sex

Touch me. Let your presence pour through fingertips, suffusing the very cells of my body with your desire for me. I will become lost to the world in my submission to you. I will forget all things to come, and all that has been, my imprisonment in this tiny mind of separation ending in the ecstatic penetration of your desire exploding within me, until this trembling mass of feeling-flesh cannot resist any longer your need to possess me.

Finally, the one I have forever sought has come to me, and this love carries me beyond not only the world of time, it carries me finally away, away beyond all I have known, all I thought could be, away beyond my self. I am dying, dying mercifully into your all-consuming desire for me, and from this hour I am helplessly, eternally, yours.

★★★★★

What can be outside the embrace of Love? Can a living, genuine, radically free spirituality be constricted against the pulsing and vibrant scent of this embodied existence, and still claim to be spirituality at all?

According to Christian metaphysics, each of us as Soul has 'fallen from grace,' but can this mean anything but that our existence here is the *very result of grace*, and thus proof of its existence? Has the Ever-Shimmering One we commonly call 'God' made a horrible mistake?

★★★★★

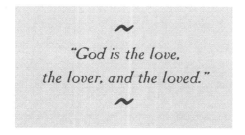

~

*"God is the love,*
*the lover, and the loved."*

~

There is no power in sexuality but the quality of Consciousness we bring to it. There is nothing it brings to us unless we begin in knowing that the lover belongs to God. Then, in each caress, every bead of sweat rolling down the spine, and in each groan emerging from being moved beyond the domain of words, we celebrate in humility the realization of every mystic lover – the sweet, ecstatic cry of a genuine, living, and radically free spirituality: *mahabud lillah:* "God is the love, the lover, and the loved."

★★★★★

There are essentially three levels of sexuality of which we may taste.

First, and by far most common: *having sex.* This occurs between beings who still sleep in the living dream of being mere bodies. Bodies groping for life, for satiation, for pleasure, for an escape from their common suffering. *Having sex* reinforces and perpetuates the ignorance and suffering of the egoic life. Resist it like the plague, for – like quicksand – it but sinks the soul into the morass of illusion.

Second, and the hoped-for goal of many: *making love.* Here, we share in physical intimacy not merely with another body, but with a person, with a sense of another's being that transcends having sex. Here, caring *begins* to emerge, and the energies of the body and its passions *begin* to do what spirituality must come to do in the extreme: crack the heart open from its self-centered contraction.

All too often, making love leads to disappointment, for the soul – still too buried beneath the weight and grip of ego – yet mistakes another as a source of something it starves for: love. It tries at this level to use sexuality to manufacture the conditions it may have spontaneously touched in rare moment of intimacy.

The mind is still plagued with all that is yet unhealed, and thus projects its unconscious *need*s onto the lover, hoping – even requiring – that the lover fulfill the deep hunger for safety, love, acceptance, and an escape from suffering that is the pervasive thirst of ego. Here, we find the attempt to cultivate technique in the hope of *making love* appear for us.

Be vigilant during this vast stage of your journey of awakening. It is a razor's edge, holding the momentary tastes of enlightenment, and the imprisoning usurping of the body yet again in service of ego.

Third, and the very rare province of sacred sexuality: *praying love*. Here, lovers come together not moved by seeking, or by need, but as the overflowing, innocent, spontaneous, and radically free effulgence which is the result of knowing that the lover belongs solely to God, and has been given as a free gift to us, so that one cannot hope for anything beyond this: that the body itself be a communication device whereby each breath, each touch, each movement of passion and power is a living prayer of gratitude for the presence of the Divine. The awakened Soul moves through the body to allow the Beloved One to be the one giving nurturance and fulfillment, and even the healing grace that a truly sacred sexuality may pour into the beloved one.

Settle for nothing less than this! Become the one first so purified in the alchemy of the Shimmering One's Fire that ego is a memory outgrown, and the body given freely to the purpose of the Holy Spirit: to share the miracle that ends time, the miracle of Love's Presence, in mad celebration of the radically free: *mahabud lillah!*

★★★★★

Sexuality is not apart from spirituality, and I challenge all views of celibacy as utterly false: mere ego-based judgments of the radiance of Creation. Indeed, a living spirituality is powerful in its fully lived passion, and neither denies nor fears the ecstasy, pleasure, and profound levels of communication and communion available, just as it does not refrain from risking the heart, nor from tears and sorrow, compassion and creativity.

> ~
>
> *All too often,*
> *making love leads to*
> *disappointment,*
> *for the soul – still too*
> *buried beneath the*
> *weight and grip of ego –*
> *yet mistakes another as*
> *a source of something*
> *it starves for: love.*
>
> ~

Indeed, Creation *is* sexual, through and through. It extends itself by opening to penetration, and by penetrating the veils of limits, does it not? For me, the Lord, my God, is a *sensuous God,* Who clearly loves to seduce with overwhelming Beauty, and reveal itself as a silky red wine pouring slowly through a human throat. And an awakened being is one radically free in divine enjoyment of his or her very existence as the presence of sexuality itself: aliveness, passion, and exactly what the heart of true spirituality and sexuality is: pure Presence, in denial and fear of nothing.

★★★★★

When you come to know that the beloved, the lover, and the love, are but the holy trinity of God's appearance, you will know the secret of the radically free, and sexuality and spirituality will be but One Divine Taste, meeting with no resistance born of the conflicts of the egoic mind.

*Touch me. Make me Your lover, Lord. Penetrate me more deeply that only You are given in the caress of these fingertips upon my lover's sacred skin, fashioned by the power of your mysterious desire to appear as Creation itself!*

This is the cry of the Soul to God, and the very energy of sexuality suffused in enlightenment, seeing the Beloved One shining through the lover, and longing to give only God to the lover: the act of *Praying Love*.

*Mahabud, lillah!*

**jayem**

*So, what jewels have you discovered here?*

# The Way of the Heart
## Prayer

*The story is over.*

*The dream of separation is ending.*

*The whole of Creation is now experiencing a growing
power, if you will, a movement, a momentum that must
carry the mind, from which Creation springs, to a new
level, if you will. It's not so much an evolutionary level as a
level of re-cognition, a level of re-membrance,
a level of re-turning. And that wave of momentum
is alive and has already arisen within your
heart and mind. You know it.*

*Stop denying it. Stop questioning it. Stop looking for signs
from the world around you that it's okay to feel it. Accept
it as a divine gift from your Creator. For the call has gone
out. And though many listen, few hear, and fewer still
become wholly devoted to responding.*

*For when you know that you are Holiness Itself, how could
you ever look upon your brother or sister and believe that
they have wronged you?*

*How could you ever want to do anything but love them?*

*That is, let the Love of Christ flow through you so
deeply and so profoundly that they get that you
do not believe their illusion.*

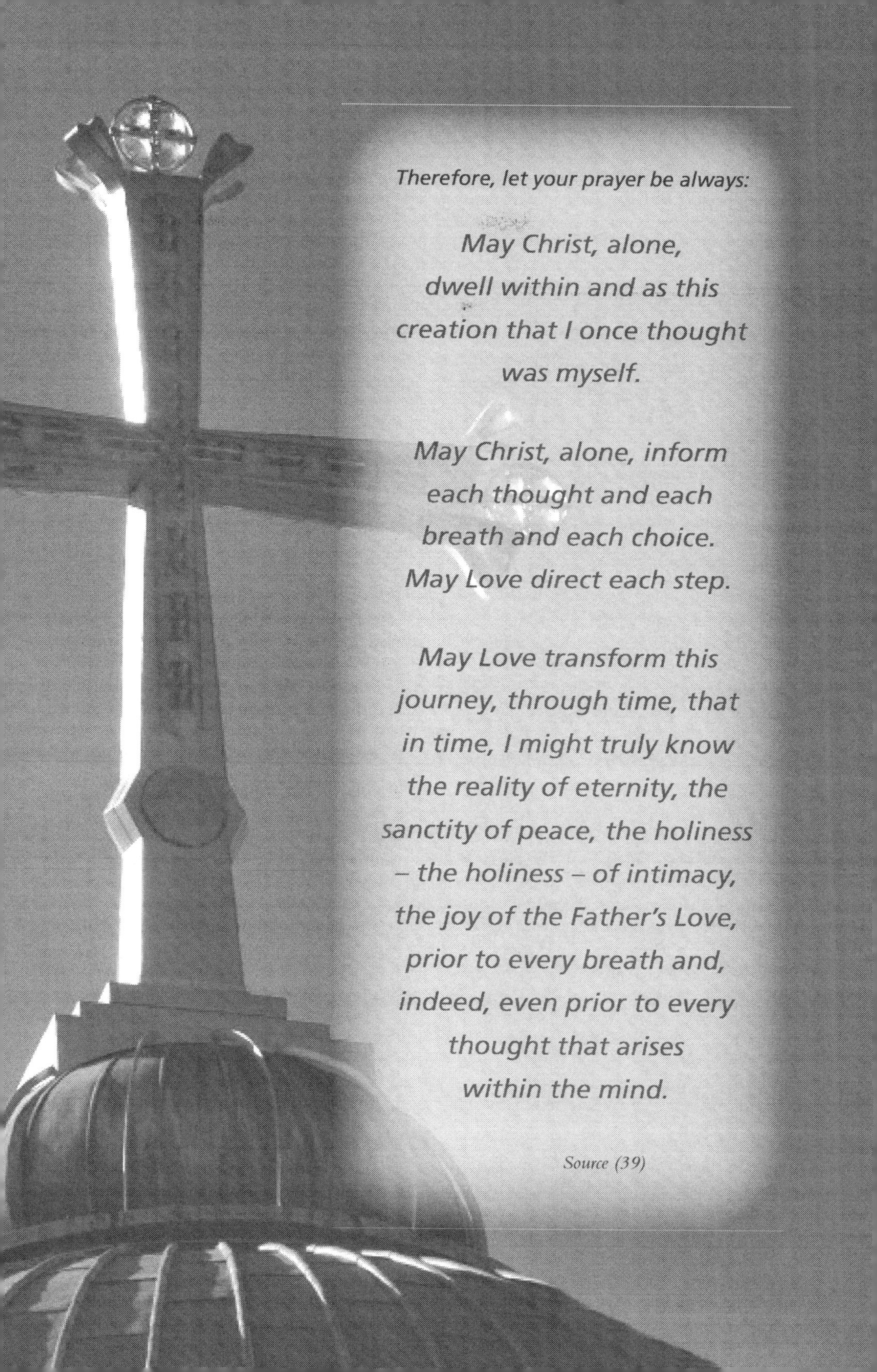

*Therefore, let your prayer be always:*

*May Christ, alone,
dwell within and as this
creation that I once thought
was myself.*

*May Christ, alone, inform
each thought and each
breath and each choice.
May Love direct each step.*

*May Love transform this
journey, through time, that
in time, I might truly know
the reality of eternity, the
sanctity of peace, the holiness
– the holiness – of intimacy,
the joy of the Father's Love,
prior to every breath and,
indeed, even prior to every
thought that arises
within the mind.*

Source (39)

Where you are has nothing at all to do
with the location of the body that you
have learned to call your own.

*Source (40)*

# Chapter 11

# The Rich Man

Recall the parable of the rich man who comes to the Master seeking entrance into the Kingdom. Falling on his knees, the rich man begs for salvation. Onlookers, assuming the great compassion of the Master, quietly anticipate His reaction: a hand placed lovingly on the man's head, a few gentle words imbued with wisdom, and acceptance of this new disciple.

The Master pauses. The crowd stills. An eternity seems to pass as He stares down at the rich man motionless at his feet. Finally, He roars so quickly and abruptly that several women in the crowd gasp in surprise:

"Go, and sell all that you own, and follow me."

The rich man looks up, quite startled, for he had been certain that the Master would be moved by his act of piety.

"Master, he mumbles, "I have worked long and hard for all that I own. Must I give up my most cherished possessions?"

The Master's gaze seems to pierce the rich man. He lifts his head to face the crowd and cries out:

"Surely, it is easier for a camel to pass through the eye of the needle than for a rich man to enter the Kingdom!"

Abruptly, the Master turns and walks away from the stunned man on his knees, who somehow knows imploring is useless. He suddenly feels very, very poor.

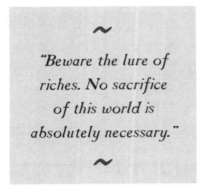

*"Beware the lure of riches. No sacrifice of this world is absolutely necessary."*

The crowd murmurs amongst itself.

A man who had been close to the scene, turns to a woman carrying a small child. She recognizes him as the part-time employee of her cousin who owns the meat shop just off the town plaza.

"You can't devote yourself to worldly gain alone. After all, you can't take it with you." Satisfied with his interpretation of what he has heard and witnessed, he continues on his way.

Near to the village well sits a man with long hair and beard. He sits cross-legged, leaning on his walking stick. The villagers had grown used to this ascetic, sitting in deep meditation in the moonlight more often than not.

"Beware the lure of riches. No sacrifice of this world is absolutely necessary." Content the Master would agree with him, he closed his eyes. The slight movement of his lips meant he was chanting the names of God he had learned in his pilgrimage to India.

As the crowd was dispersing, one man seemed overwhelmed managing three small children. His wife labored to keep up, her hand on her painful lower back, belly large with child.

The man spoke to his wife, though it was hard to tell if she was listening. Actually, it had been that way for quite awhile.

"Well, it was interesting. But the Master wasn't talking to *me*. After all, I can barely make ends meet in this dog-eat-dog world."

Dismissing it all as irrelevant to his hard life he, too, continues on his way.

The spiritual path requires steps that cannot be circumvented. Knowing this, the Master looked into the rich man's soul and — discerning what was real, but hidden — spoke the revelation of his next step.

At some point, we must go and sell all that we have. Yet, this has nothing to do with material objects. No, we cling far more tightly to especially two cherished possessions.

The second of our most cherished possessions is 'certainty': those unconscious perceptions and beliefs we have acquired on our way, like flecks of dust silently alighting on our easy chair. With these, we weave a bubble of safety against the vast Mystery of Life itself, and will often argue or even go to war (as individuals or nations) rather than allow this bubble to be questioned. The threat stirs deep fear.

Our first most cherished possession is the unquestioned sense of the 'I' who possesses certainty. That is what rests in the center of the bubble, and how viciously (though unwittingly) we will defend it.

But the Master speaks to us, saying, "Go, and sell all that you own."

We must, indeed, surrender our 'possessions,' not because it will make things better, but because nothing else can be done. This is a major stepping stone in the journey, and we know we are there when our foot lands upon it. It is a choiceless choice.

Still, fearful of the uncertainty that surrender of these priceless possessions entails, the contraction in the core of our being – often called 'ego' – recoils. It chooses some form of distraction, cleverly makes excuses, or even outright attacks whomever the Beloved may use to deliver this stepping stone to us, such as the Master.

This deception to which we desperately adhere grows yet more subtle when we declare ourselves to be on "the Path." We become unwittingly selective, continuing to operate from the same old tired state of mind: "Awakening sounds great, as long as I get to call the shots!"

After all, we may end up having to discipline ourselves. We may (dread the thought) have to struggle, and become familiar with the true uncertainty in which we live and move and have our being. Even worse, we may have to *feel* all the crap we have disowned, burying it deep into the very sinews of the body itself.

We are the rich man. Hiding our insincerity while we grip so tightly the bubble we have invested so much energy in building and maintaining, we approach the Master (who may appear in many guises), seeking Grace. Before Him (or Her) we stand naked: there is no such thing as privacy, though we may believe there is.

Faced with such profanation, the Master turns and walks away. True compassion is, and must be, ruthlessly uncompromising, for anything less will fail to transform the soul from repository of ego to an open channel for the very Mystery and Love that GOD IS.

*As I look upon my environment, if I imagine the things around me were taken away, would that take anything from me? Would I be less than before?*

*Recognition is not dependent on any specific state of body or lower mind. It is not necessary to spend endless hours in meditation seeking to quiet the mind. It is only necessary to withdraw value from what arises in the field of the lower mind, so that, quite naturally, what arises, what is recognized, is the perfect value that is held in your prior union with God. This is why awakening, salvation, or enlightenment, is not a change at all, merely a recognition of what has always been, what will always be – eternally.*

*Life has birthed you. The Mind of God has given rise to you. You are God's. You are not the owner of life. You are the recipient of it.*

*Source (41)*

Eventually, the soul that
is truly committed to
awakening does not flee
uncomfortable situations
until it believes it has
fully extracted all the
wisdom that it can.

*Source (42)*

Chapter 12

# Breathing Room

The depth of Sacredness in our lives – which is the quality of love, connection, and aliveness – reflects how deeply we have allowed the Absolute, or Love, to transform us and our relationships. As we "turn back" and bring to light all the darkness that has settled within, we begin to dissolve our self-created obstacles to the shimmering presence of Love as our true Identity. We are shocked into the direct realization that God is not far away at all. In fact, we learn that when we are truly present as the embodiment of Love in the world, we immediately have God, and God has us.

Yet few of us have been shown the way to Love. We get most of our learning from rough and tumble on-the-job training! After so many bruises, we either withdraw into a safe shell (even in a relationship) or we make the inquiry into what does not work, and slowly we begin to discover what does. This discovery always comes as a revelation, for what works in sacred, loving relationships is exactly what sages have been teaching us works in the quest for enlightenment!

Sacred Relationship requires a transfiguration of the self we have thought ourselves to be. It requires dismantling the veils we have built around our hearts to keep us safe, discovering our own authenticity and living it fully, releasing all the dysfunctional "tapes" we have acquired from our past, and cultivating the ability to truly empathise: to enter sensitively into the

*The Secret to experiencing both Sacred Relationship and the presence of God is what I call "Breathing Room." The principle is simple: nothing can flow into a space which is already full.*

soul of another, to become one with another, whether in their joy or their pain. Sacred Relationship requires the same kind of transfiguration the mystic must go through to become one with God. In both longings, we are called to surrender everything we have known, and become literally the "vessel" through which the Absolute, as Love, pours toward the beloved. Our refusal to give up our previous perceptions blocks us from realizing the highest and most fulfilling relationships, just as it keeps the seeker of God forever a seeker.

The Secret to experiencing both Sacred Relationship and the presence of God is what I call "Breathing Room." The principle is simple: nothing can flow into a space which is already full. If the "space" of our hearts and minds were filled with Sacredness and God, we wouldn't feel so dissatisfied! This can mean only that there is "no room at the Inn." That is, we have become full of something that prevents what would most fulfill us from flowing into us. If this were not true, we would have what we long for already.

I would like to offer to you the Seven Gemstones of Fulfillment. I know that if you wrap your soul around them, they will lead you in ways unimagined, into and through the land of transfiguration that alone can gift you with the fulfillment of your longing for Sacred Relationship.

# Gemstone One

What you long for is longing for you.

The journey to fulfillment of the soul begins in the recognition that the desire and longing you feel, whether it seems directed toward the longing for Love in a human relationship or toward a spiritual relationship with God, is already sacredness appearing within you. That longing needs to be as a priority in your life. Go ahead, take the plunge and state clearly to yourself your deepest longings. And then realize that this very longing is actually the way the Universe is calling to you!

Give yourself the breathing room necessary to feel your deepest longings and desires. This is the very first step in becoming capable of receiving their fulfillment.

## Gemstone Two

Harry Truman made famous the simple phrase: "The buck stops here."

In our quest for sacredness, both human and divine, we must freely choose to interrupt the ego's penchant for passing the baton of responsibility. I invite you here and now to take a deep breath and say the following within yourself, until it seeps into your cells:

*"I and I alone create my experience. All that I see, have, do, and am is by my perfectly free choice. I free the world from any blame I have placed upon it, or anyone."*

Taking 100% responsibility frees up enormous energy we once frittered away in making excuses, defending our opinions, and enlisting others in our sad, sad stories. As *A Course in Miracles* asks: "Would you rather be right, or happy?" The decision for 100% responsibility opens a magical door between what you have been, and what you can become. Go ahead. Make the space for this clear decision now!

## Gemstone Three

Be what you want to attract. In the realm of transforming the soul, receiving what we long for works by the Law of Attraction. Therefore, in your quest for sacred, fulfilling relationship, choose now to look honestly at how what you want to attract is blocked and take corrective action!

Following especially on #2 above, stop wasting time complaining about the love and sacredness you are not getting from your partner (or lack of one) and focus entirely on these simple questions:

*"How can I be more present today?*

*How can I extend sacred love into my world, right now?"*

Cultivate the realization that the mind always moves immediately in the direction of answers. Following inner promptings takes us into the experience of extending love into the world, and when we give, we immediately receive. Honor and follow your inner promptings to extend love into the world.

# Gemstone Four

What is hidden must be revealed before it can be healed. In Sacred Relationship, transparency is absolutely essential. As Jacquelyn Small points out in her excellent work, *Awakening in Time*, "If it's happening under your skin, it's yours." Use all feelings and perceptions that arise in the dance of togetherness for what I refer to as Radical Inquiry: getting to the deepest truth about our reactions. In this way, we unravel what causes us to withdraw love and presence. For example: all anger at something or someone is ultimately a veil covering a fear of something. In countless couples sessions, and in my own life, I have witnessed the miraculous power of radical inquiry into reactions arising in relationship when the primary fear is uncovered and allowed to be felt completely. It always produces closeness and connection, the very hallmarks of sacredness. Like a budding mystic or spiritual aspirant, see that all real work is the discovery of how fear has crept into our hearts and minds, usurping the place where the very Love of the Absolute longs to dwell within us.

> ∾
>
> *Transparency is a skill, easily learned and deceptively simple, yet it requires time and practice for us all, because it is the opposite of everything the world has taught us to do!*
>
> ∾

Transparency is a skill, easily learned and deceptively simple, yet it requires time and practice for us all, because it is the opposite of everything the world has taught us to do!

The commitment to master transparency leads to the deep realization of something priceless: the ability to love and be loved deeply, and the direct experience of God's Presence. In short, Freedom of the soul.

To begin creating the Breathing Room necessary for transparency to blossom, start by asking yourself the following:

*"What feeling, or fear, have I possibly withheld from my partner? Has this caused closeness, or a sense of distance?"*

Make a commitment to seek out and learn the skills of transparent, safe communication in your relationships. A great guide to start with is a book by my friends, Gay and Kathlyn Hendricks, titled *Conscious Loving*. Remember, transparency reveals all that must be healed in our minds for Fulfillment to blossom, both in our personal relationships and in our relationship with the Absolute.

## Gemstone Five

Which Universe have you been living in? If that seems an odd question, consider these words from Albert Einstein:

*"There are only two ways to live your life:*
*One is as though nothing is a miracle.*
*The other is as if everything is."*

I like to underscore this Gemstone by noting something very important about potential places for our hearts and minds to live.

In the Universe where nothing is a miracle, something threatening can happen: mistakes! When I live in that Universe, I must always be unsure about myself, and especially unsure about you. So much of our suffering can be traced to our "certainty" that the "other guy" has failed us in some way; a mistake has been made.

In this Universe, I must settle for being a victim: others "cause" my unhappiness! Of course, this is the opposite of everything our earlier Gemstones tell us! In the Miraculous Universe, there are no mistakes. All events are seen as an unfolding support of Love to nudge us toward our Awakening, and out of our illusions! Every mystic and sage has lived in the Miraculous Universe.

~

*Enjoy the Breathing Room expanding within you as you relax your body. Breathing evenly and deeply, take fifteen minutes now to do nothing but look at what is around you.*

~

*...make love, not war.*

Enjoy the Breathing Room expanding within you as you relax your body. Breathing evenly and deeply, take fifteen minutes now to do nothing but look at what is around you: an object on your kitchen table, the quality of light in the sky, or any sounds that come and go. Do you really know what these things are, or how they have truly come into existence? No!

Sages know their bliss comes from accepting the utter miracle of all things arising and passing away. Simply see, hear, and appreciate the Mystery touching your eyes or your ears.

# Gemstone Six

One popular opinion, one which in many ways literally keeps the world spinning while getting nowhere, is this: Happiness is caused by the successful arrangement of people, places and things around me. If you feel such a thought doesn't have a grip on you in some way, think of all the times you have felt unhappy, while your mind was fixated on what changes must occur in order for you to be happy! Here is the truth about happiness:

Happiness is a choice, and is literally uncaused by any external condition whatsoever. The source of happiness is in our infinitely powerful minds, and our freedom to choose.

To create Breathing Room around your experience of Happiness, ask yourself the following:

*"What condition(s) have I been placing on my truly being happy? I will be happy when _____."*

Now, imagine what you will feel like when that condition is met. Become familiar with it in your body. Then, decide to enjoy feeling that way now! Remember, in the transforming of the soul, and cultivating Sacredness in our lives, the Law of Attraction is supreme. To experience greater happiness in relationship to God, and to other fellow human beings, grow yourself into a field of happiness, and watch how your life begins to "miraculously" change!

# Gemstone Seven

Mae West was a master of this: Become the most capable lover possible and learn to see every moment of relationship as an opportunity to literally "make love, not war." To give yourself to this task is the consummate spiritual act. Imagine how our world would be if everyone practiced – in the moments of all their relationships – the mantra given to us by the 14th century Sufi mystic-poet Hafiz:

*"My dear, how can I be more loving to you, how can I be more kind?"*

To create Breathing Room for the lover in you to emerge, simply use Hafiz' words when interacting with another at least ten times a day! Also, tune into a time when you felt completely loving. Feel the feelings that were present with you then. Become familiar with them, create them now, just for the enjoyment of it, and then do the next thing life is asking of you from that loving feeling, no matter what it is!

And now, here is the deepest secret I can give you. It is the truth and essence of all gospels and teachings; the very essence of enlightenment:

*You are That Shimmering One who created your body-mind as a device through which to extend love into creation.*

Your very existence is sacred beyond all measure. Isn't it time to give up the "Reluctant Soul Syndrome" and embrace your very life with passion and honor? Would you join with me in a commitment to living Sacredness into all your relationships, while opening to Remembrance of God? You don't have to wait until you "know how." Why? Because the Absolute, the very realm of the Sacred, longs for you as you long for it. Merely making the commitment sets in motion all manner of things in support of your desire.

The Universe you may have learned to see as alien, mechanical, and separate from you, will begin to conspire – that is, breathe with you – in support of your transformation. Can any journey be more worthwhile than the one in which millions of us arise from our slumber and actively choose to bless this world with the Sacredness of Who We Really Are?

*The real question is... what is there that remains unacceptable to me?*

# PRAYERS OF THE MYSTIC LOVER:

# The Prayer of Gratitude

*Thank you, LORD, for our lives.*
*Our lives are but Your Life,*
*We ARE One!*

*For gratitude is the attitude*
*of enlightenment,*
*and praising You is the raising*
*of the soul's vibration!*

*Thank you, LORD.*
*Thank you, LORD.*
*Thank you, LORD.*

*Ameyn.*

*Source (43)*

# Stepping Stones #3

Imagine, though, a state in which there simply is no physical form, and you are abiding as Consciousness, Itself. Oh yes, you have awareness. Oh yes, you have form, but that form of energy has not condensed into the third dimension.
You have friends. That is, you have other consciousnesses with which you are in perfect communication. For the vast majority of you, in fact, we would say here in this hour, all of you are sufficiently evolved to have come into this life of yours, now, from a state of consciousness that is quite peaceful, quite joyous. Communication with those we would call as 'friends' is unbroken. It is consistent; it is respectful; it is loving; it is free.

As you relax and listen to this simple description, what color, or colors, begin to come to mind? Notice them, pay attention to them. What images seem to fleetingly flow through the mind? Notice them, pay attention to them.
For remember an ancient truth we once gave you: You cannot imagine that which you have not experienced, for imagination is the picturing in the conscious mind. That picturing must come forth from something. Mind, as you know it, can only picture what is or has been. It can then, of course, find ways, at times, to bring it back into the third-dimensional experience, but that does not mean that it is new.

As you were abiding in that state, you were in relationship. Most of you were multidimensionally aware, that is, while you had a predominant color or level of energy, you were aware that you were surrounded at all times by other dimensions. Many of you communicated multidimensionally, both with that which would be called of a higher frequency as well as with that which would be called of a lower frequency. Many of you communicated with beings who were incarnated within the third-dimensional realm.

Turn back, then, toward your creations. If there is anything uncomfortable about your past, turn back to it, examine it, feel it, look at all the patterns that made it come up... Interesting decision I made, when I was twelve, to steal my neighbor's bicycle. I remember how I ended up in juvenile hall. Hmm... What was going on just before I made that decision? What pattern was running me? Oh, my goodness! I was looking to get attention from my Dad. Wow! So the need for approval was running me. How fascinating! How is that pattern running me now? Is there any trace of it left – still needing approval of another?

You will be amazed by what you discover!

Source (44)

"If you would see
love heal this world,
remember that you
have come forth not
to seek love but to
extend love."
*Source (45)*

"No greater spiritual practice
will you ever find than the
simple practice of choosing to
remember that you are love and
that in each moment only one
thing is truly occurring: there is
either the extension of love or
the projection of fear and guilt."
*Source (46)*

"Not one thought,
not one act, not one
experience, not one
miscreation remains with
you unless you insist on
carrying it forward from
this moment to the next."
*Source (47)*

"A world that is
perceived differently
is a different world."
*Source (48)*

"One who seeks, indeed will
find, but in their finding they
will be at first troubled and
their being troubled will give
birth to a grand laughter, for
what they will find in the end
of their seeking is the same
choice that was there when
they began their search. The
choice not to seek for God, but
to recognise that love is already
the reality of your being."
*Source (49)*

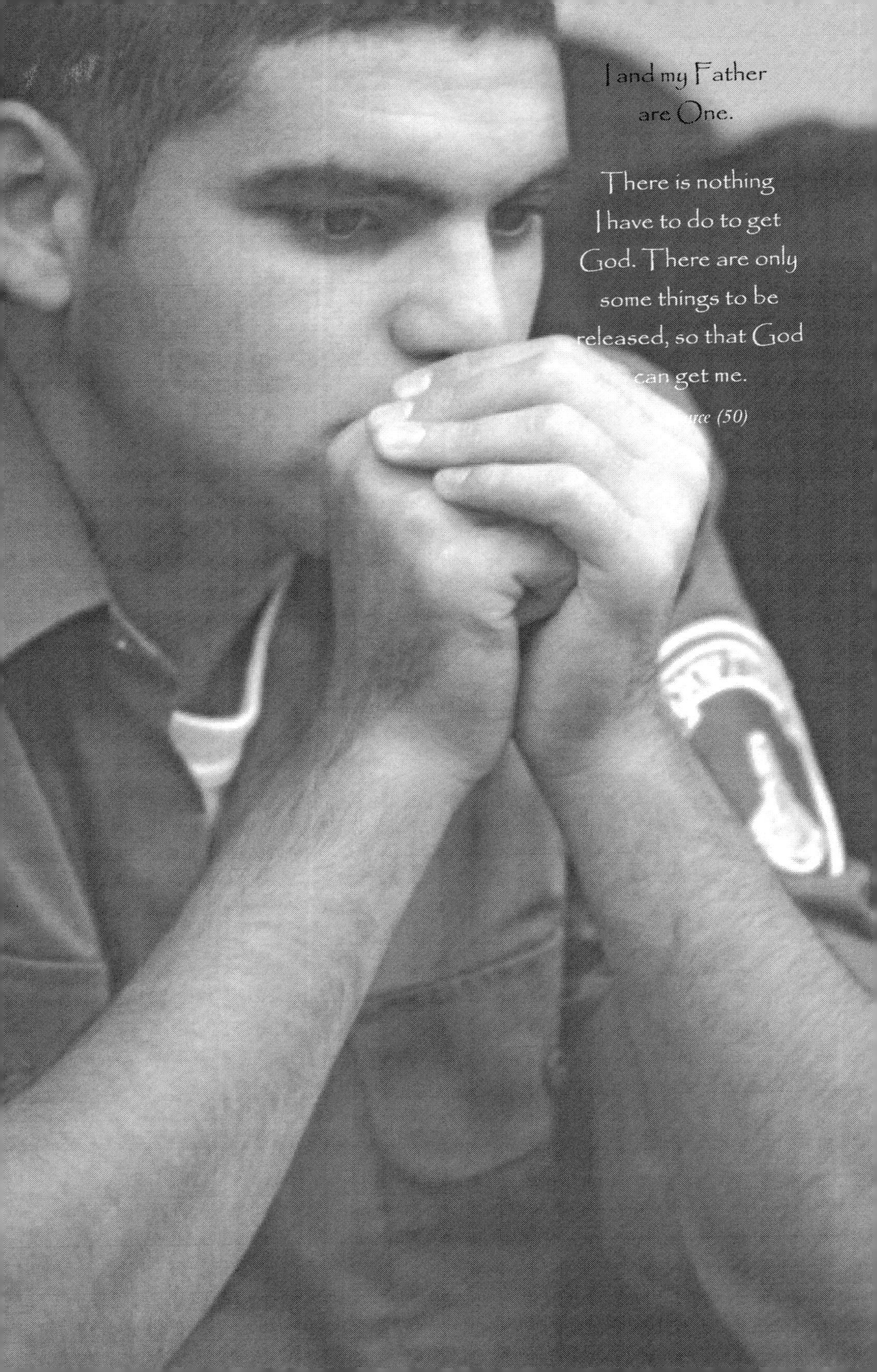

I and my Father
are One.

There is nothing
I have to do to get
God. There are only
some things to be
released, so that God
can get me.

*Source (50)*

## Chapter 13

# The Gentle Kiss of "No!"

## Walk softly, but carry a big stick

Saying "Yes" to everything is a pretty popular concept in spirituality these days. Actually, saying "Yes" to everything with one's entire being – mind, feeling, breath and soul – has *always* been a fundamental characteristic of genuine spirituality

And a hallmark of a maturing soul, that is, one that is illuminated by, and illuminating more and more real Light (as opposed to beliefs *about* perceiving oneself as spiritual) is a freer, wiser, radically liberated, even zany and passionate capacity to **saying "Yes" to an emphatic "No!!!!"**

Did I really say that? *Noooooooo*.... Oh yes, I did!

★★★★★

There is no getting around it. Spirituality is a level of development in consciousness; that is, in the capacity of Pure Spirit to shine into and through phenomenal existence, and that means you and me! It begins to emerge when, by grace, the power of consciousness itself begins to 'see through' the game of ego, or the separated self. In fact, the Latin word for God, *deus*, literally means, 'to see.' Spirituality, then, is an amazing stage of evolution in consciousness marked by an on-going 'seeing into' things. And it is equally an evolution in a mysterious process of *being moved by something greater than one's normal mind, in an ever-increasing, powerful, enlightened, and spontaneous response to what is 'seen.'*

And the movements of the enlightenment will at times, confound, piss off, and anger the flailing, myopic, self-contracted fear that is ego, desperately holding on to the tiny box in which it lives!

★★★★★

*He walked with his guru, somewhere in northern India, in the searing Indian heat.*

*Ahead, they saw a holy man — all dressed in white — followed by an entourage of disciples.*

*Now, his guru was a sadhu, who was usually naked, unkempt, owned nothing (except the peace of the radically free).*

*As the holy man approached, his guru blocked his path. If the holy man moved left, so did the guru, his shining eyes never leaving the holy man, his smile radiating.*

*"Good god, man, step aside. You smell!" said the holy man.*

*The guru (which means, 'dispeller of darkness') slid his hand down the back of his pants, and farted. His hand brought out a big, fat, smelly turd, which he held up to the holy man.*

*He and his entire entourage gasped in revulsion.*

*Then, the guru calmly took a bite, and swallowed! The holy man turned as white as his pure white 'holy man' clothes.*

*"Until you are truly willing to ask God to help you eat your own shit, how can you ever find true holiness?"*

*The guru laughed uproariously, and stepped aside, and the holy man moved hastily past, but occasionally he was seen to be looking back over his shoulder at the sadhu.*

★★★★★

Gradually, our desire to 'see into' the roots of our own self grows stronger and stronger.

Confronted by a gnawing pain within to be free, we finally submit to deeper and deeper levels of self-honesty; we shine the light of awareness directly on the crap we have been operating from. A wonderful signpost on the journey is when one can't wait for the next breakthrough to occur, and there is a spontaneous thankfulness when our ego is revealed to us, no matter the means.

Christian mystics refer to this as the grace of the ordeal of suffering. Let's face it: it isn't always (or ever?) a delight to have the universe reflect to us that we are a far cry from operating from Love!

★★★★★

There is a grave sickness permeating our world. It is a cancer eating at the soul of humanity, and if the spin talk of politicians currently occurring in the US presidential campaigns is any indication, it is reaching epidemic proportions. Here is an example:

During the 2004 U.S. presidential election campaign, Republican Senator Robert Dole suggested that Democratic presidential nominee John Kerry had received a purple heart during the Vietnam War for wounds that "didn't even bleed," implying his position as a war veteran capable of making hard decisions was suspect. When Kerry properly demanded an apology, Dole replied, 'I didn't mean to offend you!" But the damage was done. Can you 'see' the great lie at play?

Why is this an example of a grave sickness? Because *no one in Dole's own camp is reprimanding him for lying, for deliberately being hurtful, and seeking to manipulate the minds of voters.*

> ~
>
> *There is a grave sickness permeating our world.*
> *It is a cancer eating at the soul of humanity, and it is reaching epidemic proportions.*
>
> ~

You see, in politics, and in the world of the ego, what matters is winning, what matters is maintaining the status quo, what matters is being approved of, being liked; what matters is what is anathema to Spirit! And the cancer is oh, so subtle.

★★★★★

Love is an intelligent power. It seeks only healing, empowerment, liberation of the Spirit within the soul, and growth of its capacity to express, or extend, the Queendom of Heaven: that which reveals the Good, the Holy, and the Beautiful. All around us, we are moved by Beauty, uplifted by Goodness, enlightened and healed where Holiness shines through.

As we mature through the often difficult, grinding up of our attachment to egoic patterns, and come to 'see' ever more deeply just how truly Life-denying they really are, we are not unlike the alcoholic finally sobering up. Though it may sound paradoxical, especially to those living in the 'milk toast' and superficial levels of what passes as spirituality these days (hey, it's all an illusion; forgiveness means 'no worries, mate!'), the *more* we awaken by becoming gut-wrenchingly honest about what has really been running us by constantly making the Evolutionary Move (you know, pointing the finger inward, not outward at anyone), discovering why we react as we do, think as we do, wondering and inquiring into self – we discover more and more of the Self: Christ. And Christ is that Light that 'shines away darkness,' it does not get drunk with it, nor pretend that drunkenness is simply 'an illusion that is not really happening.'

Real Love is so passionate about the birthing of everyone's inherent Greatness, everyone's inherent god-self, that when it really starts to show up, it is a Fire as often as it is a warm snuggle!

When we mature sufficiently to enter spiritual Compassion rather than ego compassion, we feel the tremendous pain underlying all actions and choices – great and small – in our brothers and sisters. And we become more and more willing *to say "Yes" to saying "No!"*

You see, in spiritual Compassion, what we value is the transformation of what we have come to 'see' is actually imprisoning another. In ego compassion, we *feel sorry for them*: "Yeah, I know exactly how you feel. Men, all they want is sex. Let me get drunk with you on your bottle of "I-am-a-victim" cheap wine!"

You see, ego compassion secretly serves only one purpose: keeping the status quo of illusions in place! After all, if *you* actually begin to awaken, and stop settling for the trance you have been in, what will happen to *me*? I will have to look at my own trance-state... ugh!

★★★★★

The woman came to a session, in which I was channeling Jeshua, quite troubled. Her son was writing checks against her account, and she was beside herself.

"Why?" Jeshua asked of her.

"Well, he's my son, and I love him."

"Does he want to change?" He asked her softly.

"He keeps doing it."

*"Call the bank."*

You can imagine her shocked response. She knew that would mean it would become a criminal matter!

*Isn't Jeshua all about love and forgiveness?* Oh, yes!

He explained:

*"Beloved woman, when a soul acts in a way that is hurtful, that soul is crying for help and healing, for this is the only meaning the world can have. When a soul reveals to you that it is not willing to embrace its error, it is saying to you: 'I require a more shocking context to break this grip of fear within me. Will you help me?'*

*"If you love the soul more than you love your conception of the soul as your 'son,' and yourself as a servant of Love more than your conception of yourself as 'mother,' you will see clearly that before you is a request to fulfill a role the soul is unwilling to fulfill itself. It requires a context that can bear upon its pain."*

Take a few moments to really let the profundity of what He is saying settle in.

When I love with the love of Christ, my love for another is moved by the highest vision of their greatness. My role as true Friend is not to win their approval, to get love *from* them, nor less to require them to avoid reflecting my shortcomings to me.

As I grow in my capacity to 'see into' the subtle dynamics of how ego has operated in me, I become more and more capable of seeing how it shows up in others. And if I love them truly, I will not let them settle for it. I will expose myself, I will risk the heart, I will risk being judged, being cast away. It doesn't matter! What matters is the Compassion to serve with passion the radical, fundamental, alchemical transformation of consciousness wherever there is a willingness for growth.

For I look and behold: I see only my Self, struggling to birth itself into and through humanity. If I hold not the highest vision of my self and others, and tirelessly submit to whatever the moment calls for, I have failed to love as "the Father has first loved me."

I thank *God* for every strong *"No!"* I have ever received from others. For there I have found the greatest edges of my own on-going evolution. *For "No" is not a judgment. It is very, very often, the most powerful expression of Real Love.*

Perhaps it's okay to 'see' that often allowing another to suffer in our refusal to say "Yes," is the greatest act of Love possible, for it serves that precious one's very unique journey of evolution. And their growth is but my own. God, I love the sound of *"No!"* Real Compassion is often ruthless in appearance, moved by the benevolent presence of true divinity.

The world hasn't any time left for the Way of Denial. Neither do you. Nor I. We need each other's passionate boldness offered in what alone is True Friendship, for the Love of God.

*Where in my relationships have I adopted, "Yes," when I know deep down it was time to say, "NO"? How does that feel?*

# POEM:

# Commitment to Love

Now, from this moment on, I will no longer
tolerate error in myself. No more games,
no more dreams. I am committed to being only
the presence of Love, for that is the Truth of
who I am. It matters not the opinions of others
who are yet resisting that decision.

Yes, I accept your presence in my life.
I turn the whole thing over.
Now, each moment is dedicated to healing
and awakening the illusory sense of separation
from God that once I created in error.

I want only that which is true always.
Love is what I want. Love is what You are.
Love is what I receive. Love is who I am.
I and my Father are One.

I live! – yet not I but Christ dwells in me.
Therefore, I submit and surrender
to the Truth that is true always.
For my fulfillment comes only from allowing
Christ to be given to the world.

*Source (51)*

"We have a great God!"

Jostina, Syrian Orthodox nun, St Mark's, Old City of Jerusalem

Chapter 14

# Borne in the Grace Stream

~

*The following is a true story of miracles*

*that occurred during Jayem's trip to Israel*

*to assist with his friend, James Twyman,*

*at his Praying Peace Vigil in February,*

*2002. While many such miracles have*

*occurred during his experience with Jeshua*

*since the Master appeared to him first in*

*1987, this is one of the first he has chosen*

*to share with a wide audience.*

~

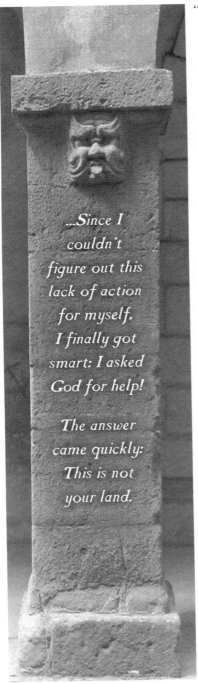

*...Since I couldn't figure out this lack of action for myself, I finally got smart: I asked God for help!*

*The answer came quickly: This is not your land.*

" I don't know why, Melea. I only know I cannot continue in this form of relationship. Something is compelling me, but I have no idea to where, or why. It would be easier if I could conjure some reason, some 'imperfection' in you, but I see only your purity, your love, and the beauty of your soul."

And so, a sweet, loving, comfortable relationship ended, and – as I drove back to my temporary rental on Maui – I cried. No, I wailed. I screamed at God, 'Why? I love M-'

But I didn't get to finish her name. Jeshua came in strongly and said:

"Do you love her enough to let her go, so that she can find the true wholeness she seeks?"

I had to pull over and stare out at the blackness of the ocean, and up at the pantheon of stars. That one moment would be the grace that I clung to as I made the journey from what had been to what might be, though I confess it was such an emotionally painful move from Melea, and from my beloved Maui, that the whole thing made me sick, literally!!

At the home of a friend in the North Bay area of California (San Rafael) I laid in bed with my body oozing 'sickness,' too weak to do much but just let go and be empty. That is when I heard the Voice of my Brother:

"Go to Ashland (Oregon) now." And so I rose and packed, and made the six hour drive.

Whenever the grace stream is sweeping me up like this, I do my best not to think, but to trust, and to look for the signs revealing support along the way. A friend in Ashland put me up, cared for me in my body's sickness, and also found me a sweet cottage in the woods to stay in, for free. Support.

For a week, I did little there but surrender. Not the kind we do hoping things will be better, but the real kind. "Do me, Lord. Use me, use me up, discard me. It doesn't matter. Nothing can take away my freedom to rest in peace, and love You." That is when it began...

★★★★★

"Hey, Jon Marc, it's Jimmy (James Twyman). Let's get together for breakfast!"

At the restaurant, our conversation turned to Jeshua. I could sense a certain resonance occurring as when Spirit is in charge of things. Suddenly, we both felt a surge of energies, and Jimmy asked:

"So, why don't you come to Israel with us?"

"Israel!" I said. "Now there's a thought from left field! When are you going?"

"Ten days," he replied.

"Ten days! Well, I suppose I could—" I had intended to say "could meditate on it and let you know."...You know, be a little spiritually chic. But I didn't get the chance.

It had been a long time since Jeshua had blasted into my consciousness with such tremendous light, accompanied by many of what He refers to as the 'Christic lineage.' Their message was succinct: *You must go!* So, the sentence I had begun changed to:

"I'm going. Now I know why I brought my passport."

"You're coming?" Jimmy asked.

"I'm coming."

We smiled, and sat in silence for a moment, both of us feeling the power of the Grace Stream in what had occurred. And ten days later, I joined some sixty other peace pilgrims on a bus from Tel Aviv to Jerusalem. Now, you must understand that, because of my many years serving as a channel for Jeshua, a lot of people had always urged me to take a group to Israel, and I had always flatly refused. I had had many insights into my lifetime at the time of Jeshua, and well knew there were places left in my soul I would rather not visit. Resistance to healing can be so deep and embedded, can't it?

For the next ten days, my body cried, laughed, danced, remembered. We baptized everyone in the Jordan River; I channeled Jeshua at the Sea of Galilee.

And at Gethsemane, I was blasted into a corner of my soul's journey long since locked away. I smelled the smells, heard the sounds, and felt the feelings of the night Jeshua was arrested. The living memory washing through me from the depth of my soul opened an old, tremendous guilt and pain. I cried uncontrollably there for a long, long time, while a blessed friend silently held my hand; a friend who was a godsend, somehow always knowing without a word when another layer in me was about to be peeled off, always there with a touch, and always conveying unspoken encouragement.

Still, when the tour ended, something was not complete.

"I don't know, Jimmy, I'm just not ready to go yet."

"Me, neither. Why don't we stay a few more days?"

Effortlessly, changes were made, and we — with four other friends also feeling incomplete — remained.

We spent one day returning to meditate in the caves of Qumran, where Jeshua had trained with the Essenes. There was an energy, a palpable presence, carrying all of us along. Later that day, at the Dead Sea, I watched Jimmy emerge and saw something mystical had occurred: Jeshua had spoken to him while in the waters. This was the birthing of Jimmy's internet course, in communion with Jeshua, called *"The Art of Spiritual Peacemaking."* Shift does happen!

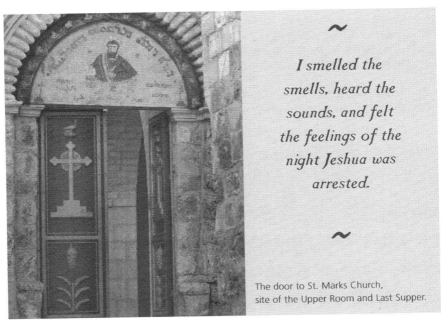

~

*I smelled the smells, heard the sounds, and felt the feelings of the night Jeshua was arrested.*

~

The door to St. Marks Church, site of the Upper Room and Last Supper.

Now, it was our last day. Something inside was calling me to be alone. I parted from my friends, and off I went, into the ancient stone streets and labyrinths, there within the walls of the old city of Jerusalem.

I did not know that we were all about to be blessed in a miraculous way, and to a depth we could not have imagined.

★★★★★

> *I did not know that we were all about to be blessed in a miraculous way, and to a depth we could not have imagined.*

As I walked aimlessly, I felt a familiar 'grating' in my heart, like something unknown stirring. I had to just keep walking, moving my body, and refrain from thinking. In the Muslim quarter, I meandered through shops, and bought things I didn't even want. Just waiting, but for what?

A shopkeeper was teaching me Arabic words for God, all the while deftly selling me more things I couldn't possibly need or want, when the grating exploded in my heart, and, in inner light, I heard God speak to me: *Go! Go now!*

I cut off the shopkeeper in mid-sentence, and ran from the store, quickly heading down the stone street, lost in this maze of streets.

*Go to the Church of the Holy Sepulchre.* We had been there once. Jimmy had shown me the tomb of Joseph of Arimathea. We meditated there, and felt the energies of this ancient place to which the Catholics later added their usual opulent version of temples. But in this maze of stone corridors, I haven't a clue where it might be. Three steps later I turned a corner, and the Church was right in front of me.

I headed to the left, to the older part, where the Greek Orthodox and (I would soon learn) an even more ancient form of Christianity prayed, a form that dates right to the time of the crucifixion – the Syrian Orthodox.

As I neared the back, drawn to the small stone and earthen-floored anteroom before the tombs, I heard an angelic voice chanting prayers, and stopped. I didn't want to disturb anyone.

Again, Jeshua appeared, and with Him were others, and their energy was both palpable and urgent: *Go in now!*

And so I found myself quietly standing near the wall, basking in the chants of a plainly dressed woman, her eyes closed, face beatific in her praise of God.

The sounds of her chants penetrated me, and some seemed familiar. In time, she stopped, and opened her eyes. And I was delivered into the hands of a human angel sent by Jeshua to guide me.

"That was very beautiful. May I ask what language it was?"

*I was delivered into the hands of a human angel sent by Jeshua to guide me.*

The woman, eyes bright and shining, replied: "That is Aramaic. The language of our Lord, Jeshua." God-bumps appeared all over my body; that quickening when Spirit is saying, "Pay attention, dude!"

I looked at her. She looked at me. Her eyes changed.

"I saw you." She said, matter-of-factly.

"Pardon me? You, saw me?"

"On my way here to pray. I went through the Muslim quarter, when suddenly the Lord made me stop, and told me to look into a shop. I saw you there talking with the shopkeeper. I asked the Lord why I was watching this man? He told me I would soon know."

Is she looking at me, or through me? There is energy running up and down my spine.

"I am Jostina (Yo-steena). I am a nun from Ninevah in Iraq." She smiled, and her eyes sparkled in some inner recognition.

"I am to take you to my church."

And so I came to be led by the hand through more winding stone passageways not yet explored. And with every step, my body is vibrating; emotion building in my heart. Then, we are there: The Church of the Virgin Mary, and St. Marks Convent.

"We speak only Aramaic in our prayers. Come into the chapel." She opens the green door, and I step into... something far too familiar.

"You can pray here alone, while I make us some tea." With that, she is gone.

I am not breathing; it's a good way to control emotion! I sit in a pew, fold my hands, and – just as my thumbs touch my forehead – explosion! A ball of energy is bursting, as tears explode from my toes up, and a veil is rent...

The whole building shape-shifts, and so does time. I am there, just after the crucifixion. Cascading memories and emotions, sounds, voices, the whole movie of this past playing itself out, welling up from soul into and through

In the Upper Room.

my present body. As it finally subsides, Jostina returns with tea, as if on cue.

I share with her my experience, and she smiles. She explains that the church dates to 3 A.D., and was built around and above the home of the mother of St. Mark, the apostle.

"Yes, I know that, somehow." I mutter. Then, her eyes changed as they had earlier.

"You know, of course, this is where Jeshua told his disciples to hide in the chaos following the crucifixion. They did so here, in the place they had held the Last Supper."

"The, the Upper Room?"

"Yes, it is here. But now it is the lower room." She explains that Jerusalem was razed in 1000 A.D. and then rebuilt, and shows me the line of old stones and new walls. Leaning forward to me, she whispers:

"You can see it, of course."

Oh, God, this is why you have brought me here. This is the completion calling me to stay, isn't it?

Jostina led the way to a stairway, and I stepped down, into the Upper Room, and into catharsis and ancient memories.

There, I simply touched a stone, and the portal opened again. I wailed. Jostina chanted her wondrous prayers, and, finally, some last vestige deep in my soul released and opened. I felt it in my lower belly, hips, and groin. Darkness dissolved, and spaciousness shone, and my heart flung open as never before.

Now, three months later★, that opening continues... but that is another story.

I don't remember leaving. Just recently, Jimmy reminded me that I had found him in an Internet Café, and he took one look at me and knew something had occurred that was big. I had taken his arm, and whispered,

"I've been there. In the Upper Room. The real one."

That night, I took our little group there, and we prayed and cried before the altar of Mary, where a painting done by St. Luke from his memory of Mary and Jeshua hangs, to which Jostina prays for healings from people all over the world.

As she shared the history of her church, and the stories of the healings, she would occasionally pause in beatific ecstacy, hand on her heart, and say:

"We have a great God!" It would become a mantra for us, now shared with audiences wherever I go.

We entered the Upper Room, chanting, praying, crying.

And even now, as I write this, tears well up. My Brother, whom I have loved, served, tried to follow, and often cursed at with a vengeance, has once again orchestrated the Grace Stream in His one-pointed purpose to awaken us all into Christ Mind. The immeasurable Love God IS had poured into space-time, and swept me up into the loving presence of my earthly angel, Jostina, and – again – I am humbled and awakened by the extraordinary presence of So Much Love.

Something is transfigured in me. Everything seems to have been swept away, both within me, and also, outside of me! I have reduced my belongings to a few boxes and my suitcase, sold my car, and – quite literally – have no plan. Just this renewed surrender in Him to passionately serve the healing and awakening of all who are ready to remember fully the Truth of union between soul and its God. To sing, laugh, dance, play, and serve. For all things are made new again, indeed.

I can see Jostina as though it were yesterday, eyes sparkling, reminding us that always:

**"We have a great God!"**

---

★ It was approximately May 2002 when Jayem wrote this article for *Way of the Heart Journal*.

# POEM:

# A Jealous God

You are a jealous lover, indeed!
Regardless of my wandering eye
and endless propensity for distraction,
You throw a lasso 'round my heart
and yank my love back to You;
each time more deeply than before.

I finally see You won't be satisfied
until every vestige of me
is territory for which you hold the deed,
free of any taint of karmically linked liens.

Then,
what will You do with me?
Will You shower me with golden kisses
raining upon my cheeks as I walk at dawn
in the mists of autumn?

Will You tantalize me with ceaseless brief glimpses
of Your sublime beauty
just as I am feeling parched by a world hell-bent
on keeping You locked out?

Will You sweep away all that I think I know,
believe I have become,
and mistake (yet again) to be mine?

Yes,
I grant it always stirs me
into the humble silence
that alone is the temple for Your lovemaking:

You like my soul perfectly naked!

*Very well, I suppose.*
*After all, You made it!*
*And solely for Your purpose.*

*It has taken me all these distractions –*
*and Your ceaseless jealousy –*
*to finally learn this simple thing:*
*There is, truly, nothing else to learn.*

*All alchemy leads to this.*
*All Your beguiling purification distills this.*
*All longing is satisfied in this.*
*All passion explodes into post-orgasmic peace in this.*

*It's true, O eternal, jealous God.*
*You are the Alpha and Omega.*
*I will go out no more from this,*
*the Holy of Holies.*
*After all,*
*Where could I go when You are all?*
*And who would make yet another dream journey*
*when the dreamer has been vanquished?*

*This is the power of Your jealousy.*
*You just don't stop until the soul is again untainted*
*by the great delusion of Me-Myself-and-Mine.*

*You, beloved God, are lover supreme!*
*You reveal what it means to give all,*
*for You have poured Yourself deeply into the basement*
*of my self,*
*then lit the match igniting the demolition*
*of the house I once built without You.*

*Thank You for loving me, my God.*
*Thank You for loving me*
*to my death in You.*
*And now You will have your way with me!*

*Oh, I see,*
*that is what You are doing*

# A Jealous God continued...

as the pen quickly scrolls these words
to be left as stepping stones for others who,
like me,
are fatefully intoxicated by the scent of Your presence
and can't help wanting more of You.

May all beings die in You, oh, precious, jealous God.
Let their souls become Your flutes,
their minds become Your harps,
and their bodies Your fingers upon the keyboard
of creation!

Throw Your lasso around them all!

But, of course, I hear You.
There's no need to ask, is there?
For it's what You do, ceaselessly.

Just let me know if I can help.
Any little thing.

Just think of it as my gratitude
for the shattering outpouring of Your grace
that answered my prayer
when I finally figured out the only one worth praying:

Destroy my illusions.
Not a single distraction has fed my hunger.
Help me to die into You.
Nothing has value but this, but I am helpless to find You.
Find me, oh God, and then,
devour me.

This prayer is the portal,
the hidden passageway that leads from death to life!

Help them to see this great death is the priceless pearl
nowhere to be found in Dreamland.

You are the Alpha and Omega,
A jealous God, indeed.

Thank God, for that.

*Source (52)*

*What if everything was being directly sent to me of my Father, because my Father knows what is necessary to unravel within my consciousness to allow me to awaken – Where am I holding back?*

*"When will you know Peace? When nothing is unacceptable to you, for you shall have chosen to wrap all things in the allowing embrace of Love, and you will know you are the freedom you have been seeking."*

*Jeshua*

And when we see through the Door of Love, Love reveals to us the precious wisdom, holy perfection, and loving Mystery of exactly what is occurring for us, and for all beings. When we see through the Door of Fear, we see nothing, understand nothing, and thus do not grow in our capacity to embody Christ. **We suffer, because in the depth of our being we know we have resisted and denied our True Self, and slapped God in the face.**

Again, we must come to see that Love is not a sentimental affection. Love is the choice for the Spaciousness in which something may change, in which our perception may be infused by the very real capacity of Wisdom that flows from the Holy Spirit, suffusing our awareness with illumination, forgiveness, and... Peace.

Now, here is the heart and soul of all genuine spirituality. It is the very essence of the Christ Path: *to cultivate the choice for Love as the Door through which we honestly enter into our own directly felt experience... especially into the seat of our Fear.*

"Whenever you know fear, or perhaps feel loneliness, or doubt, it is because you have forgotten the purpose of the body. While it is true that the body was created in an attempt to separate from God, the Holy Spirit has already corrected its purpose. And that purpose is only to be a vehicle for communicating Truth: and only Love can be True.

*Source (53)*

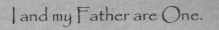

I and my Father are One.

From this moment forward, I walk and live as one who chooses to use the power of mind, the power of awareness, the power of intention, the power of clarity, the power of being itself, to know the truth that sets all things free.

*Source (54)*

At the gates of The Church
of the Beatitudes, Galilee

Chapter 15

# The Beatitudes of Jeshua ben Joseph:

## uncovering buried gems

**[Common English translation, 1: Blessed are the poor in Spirit, for theirs is the kingdom of heaven.]**

*H*e had been watching them. Many months had passed since He responded to the longing awakening in them, like the butterfly stirring to break from the shell of the caterpillar. That warm summer day, he had begun to give them the 'yoga,' the practice of attunement with Allaha. Indeed, it was the Prayer of the Lord, for it was instruction in how to enter and attune with the field of divine harmony and oneness.

*Yes, He had been watching. Some did more than simply hear Him. Some, the precious few that would form the nucleus of His disciples, left Him and actually practiced. "Why," He reflected, "is it always the women who move so quickly from hearing to practice?" He suspected many of the men followed suit, only to follow the women! But perhaps it will always be like this, for does not the Feminine stir and awaken the Masculine?*

*He silently gave thanks to His own teachers, for revealing the secret depths and the sacred value of Woman, and for the men who were following their lead, genuinely.*

*"It is not time for Woman to lead, but that time will descend upon this world as the spring rains follow the dark deprivation of winter." The end, as He well knew, is perfectly certain.*

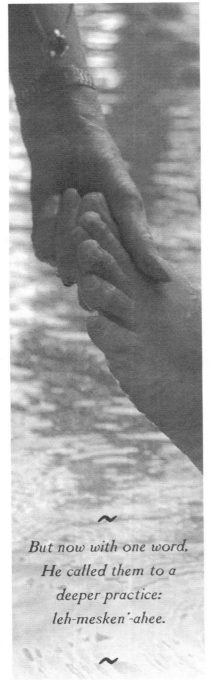

*But now with one word, He called them to a deeper practice: leh-mesken´-ahee.*

It was time. He gathered those whom He had watched do more than listen and pontificate. He gathered those whose longing hearts had stirred them to practice what He gave that day. Many had followed His advice and did so as the angel of sunlight cast its first caress upon the earth. They had understood His teaching to 'seek first this Queendom of Unity, and all things will be added unto you, for well does Allaha know you have need of these things, and the ever-Nameless Greatness will not leave you comfortless.'

It was nearing dusk. The afternoon was descending toward the night, as the angel of sunlight changed her touch to soft velvet, and the rocks and grasses seemed to glow from within. 'As they truly do, when the eyes see from the awakened heart,' He thought silently.

They began with what they had been practicing, until all could feel the vibrating unity of ever-living energy, their prayer coming to resound as one voice, one breath, one sacred event: Ah-bwoon, Ah-bwoon, Ah-bwoon… d'washmaya! d'bwashmaya! d'bwashmaya!

They were surprised when He raised his right hand in the familiar sign of the Essenes, his first two fingers extended with His thumb, the last two gently bent into the open palm.

It was the sign of greeting, and they always knew that in these times of instruction, it was the call to quiet attention. They sat, or sprawled out on the grasses, some holding hands, others resting their heads on the belly of another Friend. Men, women. Friends, of the Heart.

**"Tubwayhun l'meskenaee b'rukh d'dilounhie malkutha dashmaya"**

That is:

*"too-bway-hoon leh-mesken'-ahee bah-rooch del-oh-nay mal-koo'-tah dahsh-mahya"*

It would yet be many years before the essence of His words would begin to be lost through generations of mistranslation, diffusing the great wisdom and healing power they conveyed. Many centuries would pass before the world was ripe for their restoration. They were never meant as platitudes, but – as with His Prayer of the Lord – a practice to be enjoined. But theirs was the language of Aramaic, and so His words succeeded, conveying the Secret Knowledge, at least for those with ears to hear and the heart to enjoin the practice. For some seeds fall into good soil, indeed.

But in this day, they knew that 'to be blessed' meant a very real energetic experience of restoration and renewal: to be quickened into harmony, illumination, insight out of conflict, stuckness, and inner disharmony. It wasn't a hope, it was the *effect of practiced attunement.*

And with this first of the new Teachings, given only to those who were ready, He began to deepen what He had introduced in the Prayer of the Lord: the key was the breath! Thus He spoke to them:

*"Restored and aligned are those who re-establish their Home through their breathing in the luminous field of living energy suffusing creation. The fertile soil of the Queendom will birth their clear guidance."*

Immediately they understood that the very first move was always the same for every soul: to recognise that without inner attunement, there could be no hope for receiving the wise guidance of the Holy Spirit, the voice within that is the bridge between Allaha and the individual soul. Only with this can the mind be suffused with vision, ardor, and the heart to, in turn, bless all beings. Yes, they understood what it means to be 'poor in Spirit': to recognise the need to set aside reactive thoughts, personal agendas, and fear, and rest in dependence on Allaha.

But now with one word, He called them to a deeper practice: *leh-mesken'-ahee.*

Those resting sat up, moved by the image the word evoked within them: finding the way within to feel as though they were resting – resting in the center of a luminous circle of light and energy, an energy fluid filled with the subtle bliss and aliveness they had begun to know through their practices. But more, it revealed that the approach itself must begin with a quality of devotional attention to this circle, this living sphere of light–energy. This was not something to be done willy-nilly, but with great care, great humility – always a hallmark of what the Master taught them:

*"Why do you call me Good? There is only one who is Good, even Allaha!"*

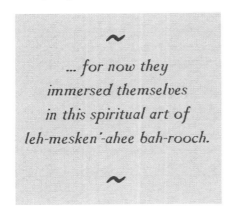

*... for now they immersed themselves in this spiritual art of leh-mesken´-ahee bah-rooch.*

He would often admonish them. Oh, yes, they had learned of the great humility utterly necessary on this Pathway.

And again that word, *bah-rooch*, from 'ruach': the inner Spirit, the breath, the living energy. This was always present in all He taught them. Discovering the power of attuning to and directing the stream of breath itself deep into the body until one could feel one's own inner energies shift and change.

And His favorite word, some would say: *mal-koo'-thah* (malkutha). Here was revealed the Feminine fertility from which all birthing comes. It always made His eyes twinkle, and often He would spread His arms and shout, *"Behold! Do you not see the birthing power suffused throughout all of the earth? Is this power not also what has birthed you? Not to wither on the vine, but to bear good fruit! Partake of it as you would a feast! And it is your very breath that brings this power to the "earth" of your own body and being, for is it not written, "And God breathed into Man the breath of life, and He became a living soul?"*

And now, he signalled them to stand and they quickly moved into the circle, with Himself a part of it, as always, for He refused of them the temptation to make Him special. And so they began, and what would later be called the First Beatitude came alive as the first step toward what would prove to be a powerful practice of transformation, unfolding its gifts in ever-deepening layers to those who learned and applied it.

They did not know in this simple beginning that He would unfold for them a Tenfold Way: ten key instructions and revelations, each inescapably linked to each other, and each one dependent upon the one before it. He would surprise them in the days and weeks to come with a whole new way to respond to confusion, or "mourning" as the Greeks would later translate it.

He would take them deep into whole new meanings and approaches to such things as *meekness, righteousness, mercy,* not to mention what it really meant to become what He surely was: a *peacemaker.* He would shock and surprise them

– many weeks hence when their practice had prepared them for it – with a whole new way to look at, and transmute even the energy we all fear the most: judgment by others, or *persecution,* that great beguiling enemy of the fully incarnated and living Soul!

For now, as the final outlines of rocks, sky, and each other faded into the warmth of darkness, for now as their inner outlines of rigid thinking and perceptions also melted into the unbounded presence of their luminous field of Oneness, for now they immersed themselves in this spiritual art of *leh-mesken'-ahee bah-rooch.* Not a phrase, not a philosophy, but a living practice, a yoga of mystical attunement to what IS, but is unseen until the inner eye awakens. 🕊️

**THE ARAMAIC BEATITUDES**

### A few important notes:

★ The Biblical Beatitudes as they have come to us were badly translated. Only in the deep contemplation – and living practice – of what they reveal in Christ's original language of Aramaic may we hope to recover the true depth and transfigurative power of these precious and high Teachings.

★ Jayem, under Jeshua's guidance, spent nearly three years in such contemplation until he realized their essential interdependence as a living practice to which all questions and dilemmas can be given. The Beatitudes actually suffuse his unique way of working with others, and of what he seeks to teach others through *LovesBreath* and *Radical Inquiry.*

★ The *Aramaic Beatitudes*: As this book goes to print a huge quickening and creative outpouring is occurring surrounding the *Aramaic Beatitudes,* which are the next step Jeshua has been asking Jayem to unfold. Jayem had no idea of the depth and magnitude that these often overlooked teachings would represent, or the major significance that they will play in humanity's future unfolding of the Christ Mind.

★ Along with the launching of the *Aramaic Beatitudes* online course, whole new levels and depths of these key codes hidden within the Beatitudes are just now coming back into consciousness. 🕊️

*The ten Beatitudes, literally be-attitudes, form Jeshua's Pathway to salvation – What are the ten benefits I might receive from exploring this pathway from the perspective of the original Aramaic form in which each was given?*

1.

2.

3.

4.

5.

6.

7.

8.

9.

10.

> *Seek first the Kingdom (Queendom)*
> *And all these things will be given you.*

*And what is the central way, for Jeshua, that we may 'seek first' the Kingdom? (In Aramaic, this comes closer to 'fertile field' or resting in a 'luminous sphere' – it's a feeling-being thing, not a conceptual-belief thing) ...* **LovesBreath** *... and nothing can deter us from this precious way of Breathing, except habit!*

*Now, here are two key Jewels of understanding relating to this most critical teaching (if you study all three books of 'The Way of' material, the essence of this Teaching oozes out of nearly every page, in one form or another!), because He is revealing to us the two key levels of experience, the union of which is Christed Consciousness:*

*1) Whenever we stop, 'turn around' through LovesBreath, and follow the Bridge to wholeness and inner silence, we access the pure field of intelligence that provides us with exactly the answer we need* **for this moment, or for our next step.** *And this is all (thank God!) we ever really need to know! Whenever the mind gets racing in its attempt to figure out, plan, or know the future and how "it" ought to get there, suffering increases. You can observe this in your own case, can't you?*

*2) But also, of such great importance, is to cultivate the qualities* **we imagine will follow** *upon our completion of our doing, our project, our task.*

# Stepping Stones #4

*Begin now to utilise some time each day, without letting a day go by,*
*in which you sit with yourself – sit with you, and start by*
*acknowledging that you are One with God.*

*Give yourself five minutes to choose, to practice choosing,*
*how you will experience sitting in a chair –*
*with a mind full of worry, or a mind full of peace?*

*Five minutes of practice sitting in a chair as an infinite creator of exactly*
*what you are experiencing in your emotional field. Sit in a chair as a Christ.*
*What would that feel like? Five minutes each day... do it without fail! Be with*
*yourself, and decide how you will experience yourself now!*

*Utilise the very process of sitting down in a chair as a symbol of preparing the*
*mind for the dropping of a pebble into it, out of which will reverberate the*
*vibrations, or ripples, that will come back to you.*

*I can sit in a chair as an Awakened Christ – NOW!*

*I and my Father are One! It's a beautiful day!*
*I've manifested a physical form sitting in a chair*
*in a corner of one little tiny dimension of Creation.*

*How amazing this moment is! I think I'll just sit here*
*and feel the heart beating in the body,*
*the breath flowing through it.*

*What beautiful thoughts can I think right now? Who*
*can I send Love to without lifting a finger?*
*I am unlimited forever!*
*I am free! I am free! I am free!*

Source (56)

All you need is Love. Love fulfills all things. Love embraces all things. Love heals all things, and Love transforms all things.
*Source (57)*

Beingness, when you look upon all things without judgment, through the eyes of forgiveness, when you decide to embody only the reality of Love, no matter what anybody else is doing, *that is when Life begins!*
*Source (58)*

When you are confronted by the Truth, you know that everything you have sought to create as a substitute for the Truth must die.
*Source (59)*

Judgment is the opposite of forgiveness. It lives on the side of the fence with fear. Forgiveness lives on the side of the fence with Love, and only Love can heal this world.
*Source (60)*

And you will remember that your fulfillment does not rest in *gaining* Love from another but in *giving* Love to everyone.
*Source (61)*

The great statue of Buddha
(Daibutsu) from Kamakura.

The great trick to
evolution, if you would
permit me to use such a
term, is to grow the soul's
awareness so that it rests
in the depth of silence,
yet does not need to
withdraw or turn away from
the expressions
of creation to do so.

*Source (62)*

Chapter 16

# Is there Life, after Birth?

I can still recall my first experience of satori (awakening), as though it were a moment ago. Of course, that is what makes the epiphanies of the spiritual journey what they are: holy instances which imprint us with what is Eternal, and eternity has nothing to do with space-time whatsoever!

I was but twenty-one at the time, newly arrived on the island of Maui, meditating six hours a day, and (to boot) getting a fatal dose of Zen Buddhism from a monk passing through. I can still feel the sudden shock of seeing, really seeing, that up until that moment, I had not even begun to be alive! It sent me reeling to see that this being I had called 'myself' was nothing but a bundle of influences: parents, siblings, schooling, culture – nothing but an effect of countless causes.

In this one flashing penetration of the Great Spell, it was clear that "I" hadn't even begun to show up yet! And yet, there "I" was, something more vast than I could have hoped to imagine, witnessing this palpable bundle of unconscious patterns, a pitiful impostor, that had been masquerading as my Self for nearly a quarter of a century. Talk about a dose of cosmic humility!

We all go through it. Better, we all enter into it, swim in it – this Great Spell of a separate self – and, if our commitment for Enlightenment carries us to the doorstep of Grace, we pass through it... into Life.

Radical truth Number One:

The problem isn't over-population: very few souls have ever accomplished the rare feat of Incarnation.

*When God said,*
*"Let there be Light,"*
*He wasn't referring*
*to celestial*
*illumination.*
*He meant,*
*"Lighten up"*

I am convinced that humanity's suffering is directly related to the shocking fact that 99.9% of births end up partially aborted: trauma, fear, and the need to survive overwhelm us in ways and to depths that require satori to even see at all; when every one is drunk, everything seems perfectly sober!

*A Course in Miracles* states, "There is a way of being in the world, that is not here." Being fully present as the Truth of Spirit is both unknown and unknowable to the world. It requires a radical reorientation of Self, or the 'Bubble of Identity' that rests as the core, or essence, of our selves.

Genuine spirituality is all about this 'relation-shift,' a death and re-birth of Identity from the ordinary view as a skin-encapsulated ego (the bodymind with a name and a history) to the extraordinary Reality of an Identity which embraces Infinity itself: Consciousness as Such or – in simple terms – the One Self God created.

From that first satori, I have traveled the labyrinths of consciousness throughout the rarefied domains of spirit, as well as the horrific depths of the shadow, only to discover that saint and sinner, Light and Dark, are but the masks of my own Self, wherever they appear.

Enlightenment is our goal, our way, and our Beginning. It is our natural, and ever-constant state. It is not so much created as recognized, and then consciously incarnated as a free act of devotion and gratitude to the Creator. So, clear principals begins to emerge for us:

1. Gratitude is the attitude of enlightenment: in all moments, under all conditions.

2. Devotion is the motion of enlightened inspiration. Every thing, everything, is transformed into the free and enjoyable act of praise. Mind is no longer directed by the need to survive, or to be right, or to get (because all sense of lack has ended). Rather, action is creative, and done only to enjoy expressing gratitude to God.

3.  Praising is the raising of the soul's frequency. With practice, it resonates more and more with the most refined vibrations of the Essence of Divinity, which yogis call Sat-Chit-Ananda: Pure Being – Pure Knowing – Pure Bliss!

4.  Life begins when I get out of the way of the Way. Since the "I" I thought I was, isn't, and never has been, Life begins when my resistance dissolves, surrendering the insane notion that "I" could ever hope to live life "my" way!

5.  I am not here to win. I am here to demonstrate that God Is, period. And only God can do that. My job, to echo the enlightened words of St. Paul, is to "die daily." (I would make that, breath to breath.)

6.  Enlightenment, Life, Incarnation, and Enjoyment are the same thing. They all require one key ingredient: Trust.

7.  I cannot find God/Enlightenment. I can only let God find me. To become fully transparent to my self is to be revealed before God, who passes judgment on the one before Him/Her: "Behold, it is very good."

8. This means I have never been right about myself. Be honest! Isn't it true that you think you aren't enlightened yet? Who's view can this be but your own? And that 'you' is a fantasy!

9.  There is only one cure for suffering the pangs of enlightenment: Get Over It! Stop struggling to live. Instead, struggle to discover Who lives, now.

10. When God said, "Let there be Light," He wasn't referring to celestial illumination. He meant, "Lighten up." For the final principle is this: Nothing occurring at any moment need be taken personally, since there is no such 'person.'

Pilgrims of the heart, rest in the Soul of your soul. Recline in the Mystery of your very existence. Dig up the tap root of your being, there, in the depth of this thing called "I" and discover Who is aware, Who is living your life now, and Who alone is the poet, the rhyme, and the reader. Look quickly: who is aware of these words, now?

Look quickly, break the spell, and be free. Returned to That One, the spell destroyed that had veiled the heart, we raise our eyes to creation and behold: God was right, after all – it (all of it) is very Good.

Isn't this what we yearn for? To be rid once and for all of this constant struggle we feel waging war within us? It is possible, you see, for there to truly be Life, after birth. If you are willing to die for it! ✍

*What conditions have I been placing on my truly being happy – I will be happy when?*

# POEM:

## Two Hearts

*Where two hearts have surrendered*
*beyond the dream of the dreamer*
*it becomes clear that only love is real.*

*Fear of loss is unimaginable,*
*and the thought of*
*possessing one another*
*is but a comedy,*
*good only for*
*a moment's belly laugh.*

Source (63)

And make not of sexuality a specialness, but rather, cultivate within it the sanctified state of consciousness in which you are deliberately choosing to set aside yourself, to let Christ love Christ.  *Source (64)*

# Chapter 17

# Sexing in God

**Y**ou might find this somewhat surprising, but did you know that many people associate sexuality with the body! It seems rather natural, doesn't it? And yet, the body is the *last level* of the expression of *true sexuality*.

What is sexuality, then? It is the very force – the creative force – of energy itself. You could say that God, your Creator, is *pure sexual energy*, since Love radiates at such a pure state of being, a pure state of vibration, so filled with *ecstatic celebration* of Its own nature that Its only function and desire is to extend itself and create like unto Itself. And what comes forth from That One, *first*, is the Christos, which means the "anointed One." This is what Christian theologians are referring to when they refer to Christ as the 'first-born of the Father,' which then comes to be incarnate *in* "our Lord, Christos Jeshua" (to use St. Paul's terms). *Christ is pure sexual energy.* Yes, I was shocked when Jeshua first began to reveal this to me, but I tell you, it's radically true!

Christos is *pure, impersonal, infinite, unbounded, universal and intelligent life force, the matrix of pure energy in perfect union with the 'Father,' or unnamed, incomprehensible Source of All-That-Is.* When matter is "anointed," or infused with Christos, it becomes awakened, en–Light–ened, aware of its true essential nature. Before this begins to occur, Nature as Mankind is sleeping, and the sense of "I" is fused to – believes it is only – matter, or the natural body-mind ('nefesh' in Aramaic).

As the Dream of Separation began to take hold in the Mind of the one Son of God (Christos) – initially as merely a temporary play, but then gradually beginning to be taken seriously – 'Christ,' as pure unlimited sexual energy, pure ecstatic Light, began to 'fall from Grace.' This means it began to descend into more and more slower, denser vibratory fields, as though a lesser vibration would 'fall' out of a greater one. Each fall, each stepping downward did not destroy the greater, just as a wave emerging from the ocean does not destroy or lessen the Ocean. At one point, energy condensed enough to create what we know as the 'Big Bang,' and matter moving in space and time emerged: a lesser whole emerging from a greater one! Finally into bodies, that Light still retains its essential nature, which is ecstatic, free, innocent, unlimited Light that is Love – and Love just loves to love. But the Light is forgotten, moved to the distant background, yet always faintly intuited. Without this intuition, no art, philosophy, goodness, or spirituality could ever arise at all!

> ~
>
> *Specialness is using a relationship to get rather than to give.*
>
> ~

All beings intuit this Light as their fundamental nature, and struggle to find it again. It is why, of all the energies that constitute human experience, sexuality is the most "charged" subject. Almost all human beings are caught in a deep internal struggle with a secret intuitive love and desire for it (which is to intuit and desire the essence of our True Self). But now, fear emerges from this forgetting of Immortal, Impersonal, Unlimited Light; identity becomes reduced to Mortal, Personal, Limited body-mind (ego). Just as what we view ourselves to be is a pale reflection of Who and What we Really Are, sexuality is "stepped down" to be only a pale, distorted reflection of what it really is. The body becomes a device for attempting to **get** a moment of release or ecstasy **from** sex, or to fulfill the secret wish for someone to provide what we believe we lack. At its worst and lowest level, it is seen as a necessary evil for procreating more bodies.

Sexual energy is creative energy – that's all. All attempts to control, repress, or deny it, kill life itself. By the way, celibacy is not about refraining from sex or suppressing sexual energy in all its variations: fantasy, desire, longing, body energies making nipples hard and penises the same! Celibacy is the spiritual art of mastering the ability to 'orgasm inwardly'; to transmute the tendency of the body to dissipate energy outward in orgasmic collapse, into an energy that explodes within, igniting a lightening bolt of energy that pours into every cell, and allows the high ecstatic frequency to be maintained so that the 'two become one flesh.' It is pure meditation, and in all spiritual traditions, the essence of meditation is Divine Union. If you have read the *Da Vinci Code*, you were introduced to the practice of *hieros gamos*, a suppressed tradition dedicated to achieving this use of sexuality in a 'yoga' to effect the awakening, the 'christ-ening' of our nature in Divine Union. In the east, this is referred to as an aspect of *tantra* yoga.

★★★★★

Sexual energy is the desire of Love to express and extend Itself. Within the body's use of sexuality, the best place to start transforming and awakening your sexuality is to learn to take what I call the 'pause that refreshes.' It is actually direct guidance Jeshua gave me when we entered into the phase of my own transformation of sexuality, and boy, I had most certainly misused it on more than one occasion!

When heading down the stream toward the ocean of sex – whether with another or by yourself, since masturbation is just fine as long as it's with someone you love! – stop, breathe, and say:

*I accept you as you are and I behold your innocence.*
*I elect to allow this body to be utilized in such a way to express*
*this simple Truth, in nurturance and honoring of*
*who you truly are: free, infinite, ecstatic Spirit.*

If sex is used by a mind *fully committed* to transforming from egoic to awakened being, the body and its sexuality *can* become the context through which Love helps to dissolve fears, self-unworthiness, and certain perceptions that have settled, or crystallized, in the mind of your brother or sister. **The body cannot be used to get anything. Its only sane purpose is to extend or give – that's all.**

The purpose, then, of sexuality and the body is *not to seek pleasure*, but to allow transformation and healing of illusion, and nothing can match the ecstasy and pleasure of that! Because the body is the ego's home, and sexuality has been usurped by the ego for improper purposes, if you will, sexuality and the body are the place of great power. A great catalyst can come through those energies, but also great risk, because it stirs up the most fundamental places in the self where the ego has tried to suppress true creativity, and tried to take it over as its own. (Ever wanted to possess the person with whom you have great sex? Ha! That is ego's voracious appetite for getting, not giving!)

This is why sacred sexuality requires, absolutely, training in being present with feelings, the ability to presence with and truly hear another, the cultivation of transparency and vulnerability, and conscious communication. If you have ever tried to go into a yoga pose, and found the body shaking,

~

*For all the men*
*who may read*
*this, if you*
*really want to*
*be blessed with a*
*penetration of a*
*woman's deepest*
*gratitude and*
*love for you,*
*transmit to her*
*the reality that*
*you are only*
*there to honor*
*her, to surrender*
*in devotion all*
*of your power*
*and passion*
*as vehicles for*
*gifting her with*
*the love of God,*
*given freely,*
*with not one*
*iota of greed,*
*possessiveness, or*
*'getting off'!*

~

and wanting to pull out of it, how much more skill and determination and willingness does it take to stay fully present to the transformative power of sexuality, dedicated to giving and not getting – celebrating the other as a sovereign being with no need to own or possess them, and remembering God as the spaciousness from which every gesture arises!

Sexuality, in an awakened state, would be entered into only as the result of prayerful appreciation, *not of the other, but of God*, so that the body relaxes and is surrendered into the Awakened Mind, that then allows the Holy Spirit to inform how another is touched, how another is spoken to, as well as how sensitively another is received... always *in*formed from the perception that the mind is seeing in the other their perfect innocence and is expressing its acceptance, its whole acceptance, of the other – not in order to *get*, not in order to *own*, not in order to *be pleased*, not even in order *to please*, but only to *express* the *innocence* of Love.

In summary, *Sexuality is God* – pure and simple. It gets convoluted in the dream, as the mind separates itself and takes on fear; as it begins to see the body as real and begins to try to use the body in order to 'get,' instead of as a communication device for allowing the Holy Spirit or the Christ Mind to express through it that which brings healing to the Sonship.

Can sexuality, then, be used in a sacred way? Of course! A pencil can be used in a sacred way. It is the *mind* that decides the *purpose* and the *value* of all things. To decide to use the sexual energies of the body only as that through which the Holy Spirit can touch another mind and heart and let them relax into self-acceptance, because they are seen and appreciated for *themselves*, and not because there's someone trying to get something from them – this is the highest use and value that the body's sexuality can have.

And, by the way, anything *but* that – *anything but that* – is a decision against Christ, and immediately brings you suffering, for it reinforces your own denial of your True Self. It results in guilt, and guilt is the great cornerstone of Separation.

For all the men who may read this, if you really want to be blessed with a penetration of a woman's deepest gratitude and love for you, transmit to her the reality that you are only there to honor her, to surrender in devotion all of your power and passion as vehicles for gifting her with the love of God, given freely, with not one iota of greed, possessiveness, or 'getting off'! Women feel deeply what is really happening, despite your words and smiles. Learn to want to give God more than to give in the hope of getting. Nothing is more fulfilling to male sexuality than to be gifted with the deepest love of the feminine, and this comes only, *only* when – perhaps for the first time – the precious woman is gifted with devotional presence that *does not seek to get or take from her.* There is nothing more painful and sad in the soul of a woman than to intuit at subtle levels that she has been used for sexual release. For it means she has *not been seen as she truly is.*

And for men, the greatest gift a woman can give is to learn how open to be *fully penetrated in every cell by the power and passion of the masculine.* To let go into full, unbridled, uncontrolled, ecstatic penetration. This is what a 'liberated penis in service to God' offers, and what a 'liberated vagina in service to God' receives, *and thus offers.* Persona drops away, then bodies are forgotten, and all that remains is Shiva and Shakti, god and goddess, the polar dance of one soul in living praise of the presence of God.

~

*For men, the greatest gift a woman can give is to learn how to open to be fully penetrated in every cell by the power and passion of the masculine.*

~

There are two terms that form an essential key unlocking the doorway from egoic sexuality to sacred sexuality. Those terms are: "specialness" and "holiness." The ego believes that sexuality is what creates the holiness of the joining of two. It's upside-down thinking. The lesser never generates the higher – never! Holiness requires not a movement. It requires a surrendering of illusion within each of two minds. Holy relationship, whether it expresses in the sacred song of sexual celebration or in eating a pizza, occurs when any two beings look within themselves: that is, they make the journey within and discover the Truth that *there is no lack*. *Then* they join, not to *get*, but to *create* the *good*, the *holy*, and the *beautiful*. That might be a pizza. It might be a retreat center. It might be what you call "making love." I don't like the term "making," by the way. That's what the ego does.

I have previously delineated the *three levels of sex* – having sex, making love, and the final is what we are discussing here: *praying love*. Here, all action is *in*formed from a different place of consciousness, from the remembrance of God, and the devotional gesture of wanting to give God to the beloved.

Specialness is nothing more than the attempt to use relationship – with a pizza, with another body, with a brother or sister – to *get*. Sound familiar? It's what we do a million times, until we grow tired of the suffering and the failure of this abysmal strategy!

Holiness doesn't mean that everybody lives in a house all by themselves and nobody is in a committed relationship, because in *holiness*, the Holy Spirit

*...the three levels of sex – having sex, making love, and the final: praying love.*

*in*forms the purpose of the relationship moment to moment to moment to moment. And if it looks like it's appropriate for two to come together and live under the same roof, even as man and wife... that *form* is *secondary* to the *content* that each mind has awakened to. The form, being secondary, can be easily embraced, and it can be easily released, when the content calls for the reshuffling of the cards. Specialness would speak thus as the 'reasonable, common sense' in the lower mind:

> *"No, now that we're together, the form is what matters.*
> *I am yours and you are mine. (Oh boy, I am special!)"*

The ego loves form, for it believes that form can give it the safety it needs while it tries to survive in its fears, secretly hoping that the form will supply the missing content. Do you see? This is why the ego can become so vicious when a relationship 'fails.' So much anger, and damage done, often for years! And why? All because the ego is bitter that its secret agenda — to make another a source of what only can be awakened to within oneself — failed. This failure is projected as a fault of the other, is it not?

By contrast, the mind awakened to holiness is *fear-less*, and only loves. And so, form has become secondary to content. Love is extended *only* in support of the sovereign growth and flowering and awakening of the beloved one, freely, with no secret requirements for a 'return on investment.'

The awakened mind no longer confuses form and content, and sees that all forms are temporary, like an artist's brush, and when it has reached the limits of its potential for extending love in the support of the flowering of Christ Mind into and through the beloved, it easily releases that form, without regret. It wonders only, "Who's next?"

This is the depth of freedom and trust and peace that comes to the awakened one. When there is nothing to get, because one is returned to God, there is nothing left but what was there 'in the beginning': Love, ecstatically giving of itself to heal, comfort, nurture, bless, and help set free the imprisoned soul of another. And I emphasise the word *free*.

If we cannot, or will not, give our beloved absolute freedom in all things at every moment, it is not love we are experiencing. It is selfish greed. We essentially have them in our life to feed off them, not to feed them. At best, we are part of a "mutual benefit" arrangement: "I'll give you this if you'll give me that. I won't remind you that you are settling for being less than you can be, if you won't remind me I'm doing the same. I'll give you security if you give me companionship. Be my little woman and stay away from others, and you can stay at home and knit! Provide me my security and only you will get my sex!"

> ~
> *There is Life,*
> *and Life is Love,*
> *and Love is God!*
> ~

Here are some wonder questions you may find useful to bring awareness to your own journey (and I honor the courage of anyone seeking to transform sexuality!)

Are you making of the body and sexuality something "special"? Or can you give even this to the sacred holiness of the purpose the Holy Spirit would give unto it, and value it so highly that you will allow *no other use of it* to enter into the sphere of your experience? That each joining with a friend, with a brother or sister, is a sexual experience; there's an exchange of energy going on. There is Life, and Life is Love, and Love is God! Can you bring such presence to sitting across from a friend and smiling while you're eating a pizza, so that *you* know you're having a grand sexual experience? You're in the *ecstasy* of knowing that Life is good because goodness is of God!

And if you happen to be engaged in the groping and the touching and the stroking and the copulating and the panting and the heaving and all those wonderful things that happen when bodies are played like lutes until beautiful music flows, can you bring that presence together so that the two are joining as though they are the Awakened Christ, serving no other purpose than to bless the other with acceptance of the other? Two beings who have chosen to 'seek first the Kingdom,' by relaxing into the remembrance of God, seeing their perfect innocence, *celebrating* the innocence of one another, without clinging, without possessiveness, without fear of loss? For where minds have joined *in Love*, loss and separation is no longer possible.

Master this art in sexuality and you will find a pathway to liberation. For when the deepest energy that gives physicality the only life it has is released from the grips of ego, and is allowed to be fully felt, loved, appreciated, and skillfully extended only as a celebration of giving God to God's child – with no trace of grasping, clinging, or need to possess – you will have incarnated the self-evident proof that God is Love, by *being* the Love of God, ecstatically using form (in this case, the sexual, sensual, and communicative abilities of the body and its subtle fields of energy) to give itself away to Creation.

"For no greater love hath any soul than to lay down your life for a friend."

When next you express through sexuality, go ahead. Lay down your own life, first. Give up wanting, needing, and manipulating, and grasping. Just relax into the ecstatic peace of letting the body be a vehicle for giving away the love of God.

And when any two, (or three, or ten, or any number you want) are all doing this in the mysterious dance of holy relationship, the Light will dazzle you! You will barely be able to handle the frequency of joy that is your secret hope, anyway. The ego's way to find joy produces only further separation, guilt, frustration, and futility. God's way opens the soul into Infinity, and self awakens in remembrance of its True Self. And all things *are* 'made new.'

And, after all, is not this perfect and only freedom – what you have always intuited as possible, what you are incessantly seeking – is not this what you want, truly? Why do you continue to settle for less, by insisting both you, and your beloved, be less than you truly are?

Set each other free from ego's merciless grasp. Be the love of God, and immediately you will know God, not as concept, belief, or hope, but as the living reality of God's immediate presence.

All of our suffering in sexuality and relationship is the result of the chronic habit of believing we can yet get from them what we continue to insist we lack. Meanwhile, the Truth waits quietly upon our welcome. We lack nothing, except giving up the attempt to constrain the extension of Love and the insane dream that specialness can provide what exists only in holiness.

When you can watch your 'dearly beloved' awakened into ecstatic love while praying love with another, and eat a ham sandwich leisurely, your breath flowing openly and smoothly, amazed at how much Love there really is in this universe just waiting to be celebrated, delighting in and feeling this Love course through you, too, as you sit with your feet propped up at the end of the bed, you will know that something deep inside has been released; an old chronic contraction has dissolved. Nothing to get, nothing to possess. Everywhere, God. And God is, Love. ✍

~

*"For no greater love hath any soul than to lay down your life for a friend."*

*When next you express through sexuality, go ahead.*

*Lay down your own life, first.*

*Give up wanting, and needing, and manipulating, and grasping.*

*Just relax into the ecstatic peace of letting the body be a vehicle for giving away the love of God.*

~

*What actual changes must I make to open myself up to extending Love through my sexual behavior?*

# POEM:
# The Best of Sex

May we all discover
that the only way to love is to
cease insisting on control of our lovers.

Let us all be shaken from the grip of the Imposter
by our unbridled passion
as Love seeps finally
into this
frenzied and sickened world
of fear.

In this way,
we may get some idea
of how the Beloved longs to love us.

You see,
the only way to know That One
is to love as That One first
loves us.

Control and calculation get only a grade of 'C'
while Appreciation, Acceptance and Allowance
get 'A's!

Someday it will be this way for everyone, you know.

And Heaven will have landed upon
this earth.

*Source (65)*

# Stepping Stones #5

*Look well, then, and ask yourself this:*

*Who do I know in my existence whom I have judged, and locked into a certain box, and I have decided that is all they are?*

*There you will find a fruitful meditation for the remainder of your time until we begin that which will be called The Way of Transformation. In other words, you have about thirty days to take the time, and use it wisely, to allow the names, the images, the faces of those that you've done that to, to let them come back to you, to say,*

*"You know, mother, father, ex-mate – whatever it is – I get it. I've placed you in a box and thrown away the key. You're stuck, so I have said. And now, I release you, that I might be released."*

*And contemplate their image. Allow the memories of the experiences you have shared with them to come back. If there are feelings, by all means let yourself feel them. Gaze upon them, in your mind, until you feel that sweetness that dissolves the imprisonment into which you've placed them. For as that imprisonment begins to melt, you will sense and know that your freedom is blossoming.*

*You cannot take fear into Love. You cannot take judgment into forgiveness. You cannot take limitation into unlimitedness. These things must be released at the level in which they were first created. Therefore, make note that this practice should not be overlooked. Give yourself thirty days with the goal to truly go back and – shall we say – mop up any forgiveness or releasing that you need yet to do.*

*Don't let the mind say,*
*"I don't know if I did that well enough."*

*For understand, it is the Comforter that releases you and the other, through your willingness to allow it to occur.*

*Source (66)*

When you have experienced, in relationship with anyone or anything, a moment of bliss, a moment of a peace that forever passes all understanding, a moment of fulfillment so sweet and so sublime that no word could touch it, much less express it, what you have experienced is only the flow of the Love of God through you.

*Source (67)*

Heaven is present, if I will remember who is making the tea… Christ is.

*Source (68)*

In the end, then, of all seeking, you must look into the mirror and decide to be the one who heals himself/herself.

*Source (69)*

But the wise gardener, who has softened the soil, who has reached in and begun to pull up the roots, to sift the soil and make it soft and open and porous, with the intent of bringing forth a beautiful garden, will indeed, then, be assisted by the Rain of Grace that falls gently, without it being earned – it is given freely.

*Source (70)*

Forgiveness is an act through which you learn what Love is, that carries you into a transcendence of the world.

*Source (71)*

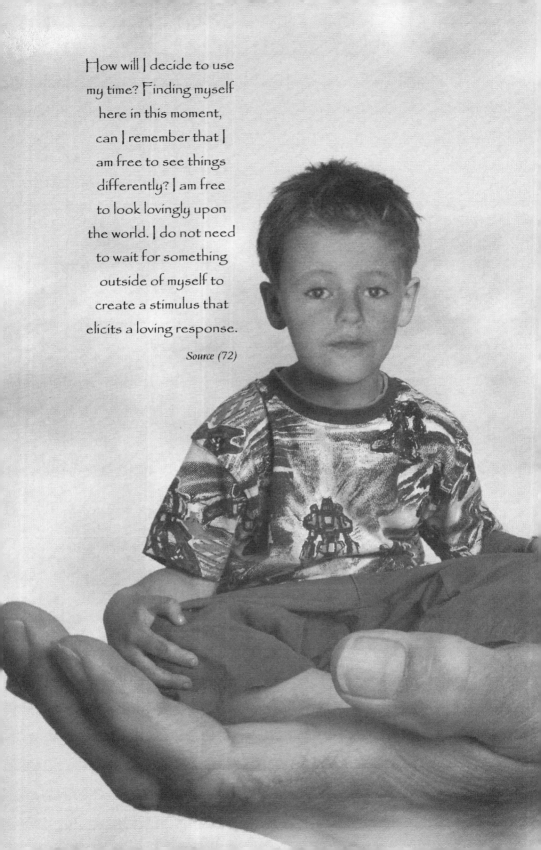

How will I decide to use my time? Finding myself here in this moment, can I remember that I am free to see things differently? I am free to look lovingly upon the world. I do not need to wait for something outside of myself to create a stimulus that elicits a loving response.

*Source (72)*

Chapter 18

# The Curse of Enlightenment

O h, yes, how much we say we want it. It's the center of attention now, at all our parties, replacing the panacea of politics, or investment vehicles, or the problems with our kids (or parents!)

We gather at our gatherings and chant wonderful mantras together, and share our his-tory or her-story, enthralled with it all to the last drop.

Without, perhaps, recognizing that we do so, we are constantly trying to re-frame the Voices of Enlightenment (all those saints and sages) so that what they say to us might be used to help us attain our *real* goal. You know, the secret one we have been serving all along: *getting what we want.*

When presented with genuine transformative practice, the kind that does not console but confronts and threatens to shatter the deeply embedded tentacles of our secret goal, we mutter ungraciously (and often project on the teaching or teacher): *But what's in it for me? And when will I get it?*

We translate everything offered *downward*, rather than face the Herculean process of giving ourselves over to what will transform us *upward*. Yoga becomes a means for better health and slimmer waists or improved cardio efficiency. Tantra becomes the next great hope for good, for *really* good, sex. Meditation is a way to reduce the stress accumulated as we race toward our personal goals.

~

*There are fundamentally two Spheres...*
*One is known very well... The Second is entered by a smaller number of beings, yet it remains inevitable that all beings enter it.*

~

Artwork by David Andor

But that is what Ego does. Everything is eaten up and digested in service of its own insatiability. And – ego being what ego is – of course *none of it ever satisfies.* We become disgruntled with this Teacher, or that Teaching, and boy, do we ever have a litany of reasons!

Unwittingly and constantly sipping on the bourbon of Separation, we clearly know where the problem lies: *out there.*

There are fundamentally two Spheres in which one can seek the end of suffering. One is known very well. Rather, it is *utilized* by the vast majority of us, but only when it is just about exhausted is there a rudimentary glimmer of seeing through it, and thus finally coming to know it in any real sense. It is here that the Second Sphere begins to be noticed at all, although it has been obviously present all the time. This Second Sphere is entered by a tremendously smaller number of beings, yet it remains inevitable that *all* beings enter it.

## THE FIRST SPHERE

The First Sphere itself has essentially two components, or gestures of appearance. The first of these is what we call the *World.* You know: secularism, materialism, family, nation vs nation, football team vs football team, special love relationships, and so on. This component is characterized by the energy of *acquiring* (and then the fervent attempt to hold on to it, whether it be lover, family, money, career, or belief system, etc.)

The second component of the First Sphere is what we call 'religion,' in any of its forms. Here, we adopt a certain untenable perspective from which we cling to an unprovable and fiercely guarded perception of IT. You know, what IT is all about, how to approach IT, and especially what to do to appease IT, so that — someday, 'god willing and the creek don't rise' — we will finally get to arrive THERE, in the 'land of milk and honey.'

Immersed in one, or sometimes both of these components (I mean, why not? Hedging one's bets seems prudent, doesn't it?), rarely do we stop long enough to look into what we are doing. There is something we desperately want, something we desperately seek to acquire: *we want consolation.* We want something to unwind our knots, and stroke our opinions of ourselves. We want love, the bourbon that can temporarily drug us, and stave off the inevitable, horrifying look into our constant suffering, our constant (though hidden) insecurity, our bazillion fears, our neurosis, playing like a movie in the 24-hour theatre of our minds.

And, oh how skillful we may become in either, or both, of these components of the First Sphere. Because both involve preserving, cherishing, and consoling the separate self, they share the need for *Time. And Time deludes us into thinking we are making progress.*

Until the hope for progress in Consolation finally begins to wear thin, and we begin to taste the exhaustion of our hope in our personal version of the Dream of the Dreamer. (Note: you may want to reflect for a period of time in this manner: 'When I dream, who is Dreaming?' How can I be certain my 'real' life is not simply another form of Dreaming? Even if I assume it is, just who is doing the living of 'my real life'?)

This exhaustion comes when it comes, much in the same way as a snake sheds its skin: at just the moment it does, and not sooner or later. For it seems to be a shocking revelation, impossible to comprehend *until* the sweet and grace-filled Moment of Exhaustion is tasted, that — like a locomotive careening down the tracks with no brakes cannot be stopped until it runs out of fuel — there is just no way 'I' can simply choose to enter the Second Sphere. Even if I try, I won't stay long, and will leave muttering something about the 'heat' in that Room!

You see, the Second Sphere is as far from the First as the East is from the West, and up is from down, and yes is from no. They are so radically different that they have absolutely no point of connection, and there is no hope of blending them.

# THE SECOND SPHERE

The Second Sphere is the province of Genuine Spirituality. It serves only one purpose: awakening from the Dream of the Separate Dreamer itself, and this is very, very different from any and all forms of *improving* the Dream, *consoling* the Dreamer, or even getting on better terms with it so one feels more comfortable in the insatiable game of seeking to acquire consolation and love. (And love, in the First Sphere, is really but a faint echo of itself used solely for acquiring consolation.)

Listen to these words, and see if you can begin to hear them:

> *To study mysticism is to study the self.*
> *To study the self is to forget the self.*
> *To forget the self is to be one with all things.*
> *To be one with all things is to be enlightened by all things,*
> *And this traceless enlightenment continues forever.*
> **- Dogen**

> *You will come to realize in due course that your glory*
> *lays where you cease to exist.*
> **- Ramana Maharshi**

And these, from my 'main cosmic guru-squeeze,' Jeshua (Jesus):

> *There is the journey to the Kingdom, indeed,*
> *but only when seeking is dissolved in the radiant splendor*
> *of having been found,*
> *does the journey within the Kingdom begin.*

Mysticism is the 'Pure Land,' the *sine qua non*, the Beauty of beauty, the Prize Catch at the top of the ladder of human evolution.

Only, you can't catch it, as much as be caught by it. And one discovers, radically, shockingly, that you cannot reach this Pure Land, for you are in it, even now.

The trick, you see, is *to see*, to finally, unequivocally see, as when you are shocked into waking by a sudden loud noise out of an entirely enchanting dream. It takes a moment or two (or even a lifetime) to get over the disorientation! The traces of dream may seem to linger and even 'catch' you as you fall for a moment into daydreams.

Seeing is an act of awareness. And God is seen only when there is no 'I' mediating the seeing, dividing it into the province of a perceiving Subject, and a perceived Object. God conceptualized, is not at all God. The God 'known' is a false God. This is the ceaseless cry of the mystics, a clarion call to you to not settle for second best!

If this all seems confusing to you, so much the better. As Jeshua reveals to us in the Beatitudes (only seen when viewed through the prism of his native language of Aramaic):

*Restored shall be those who allow emotional turmoil, and are confused. They shall find their new home in universal power.*

Confusion is a breakdown of what has imprisoned us, a prelude to break*through*, if you have the fortitude to want God so badly you will desire Her above all known and created things, and be willing to allow your little self to be utterly destroyed and shattered in Radical Freedom. ✍

~

*Restored shall be those who allow emotional turmoil, and are confused. They shall find their new home in universal power.*

~

*How deep is the tiredness with this world I reside in? How much of God am I willing to receive and allow to be expressed through me each day?*

*Jewels of the*
CHRIST MIND

*"A Master is one who knows
they are always a student,
and is dedicated to being
the very best possible."*

*Cultivating the artful skill of studentship is one hundred percent
absolutely essential for the Christ Path! Here are a few qualities of it:*

- *perpetual Wonder*

- *willingness to be wrong, and enjoyment upon discovering that
  you have been*

- *thirst for God*

- *confession of one's ignorance*

- *recognition of utter dependence on a Higher Source (Holy Spirit)*

- *Equality of Innocence (how self and others are seen,
  no matter what)*

- *humility*

- *forgiveness (the best place to practice is with oneself!)*

*One of the key jewels is the constant need for vigilance against
the egoic trap of thinking "I already know." That is, taking the time
to return to the beginning, over and over and over, for the hallmark
of the good student is complete non-resistance to being taught.
As we cultivate the artful skill of studentship –
as we discover how to be 'happy learners' – something happens:
Christ Incarnates into the space once all clogged up with 'me'!*

*Source (73)*

# Mystic Fool

Seekers are constantly involved
in all manner of ritual and debate
ever hoping to catch a glimpse of the Beloved.

But the mystic who has been ravaged by Her
simply embraces each moment
and is devoured anew by Her
over and over eternally.

Having thrown away the Imposter,
there is no more striving, no more seeking.

Here, the fruit has ripened:
the Lover in us awakens.

Reject nothing!
Allow this transient existence
to be transformed
through your unobstructed feeling-embrace.
Ask only to be devoured by the Beloved
and She is immediately revealed.

But we have secretly wanted
anything but Her,
and so have stored up sad dramas
or clung to the false hope of security
for tomorrow.

How will we find G-d
if we do not submit to loving as She loves?

Hear now this:
**Love does not condemn.**

Resisting this no longer,
the Imposter slips gently into
enlightenment,
as a dew drop slips into the ocean.

Arise, mad lover.

Source (74)

The servant *trusts*.
Embracing all things,
having given the world up to his Father,
he is content in *this* moment
The whole is present in the part,
and the part embraces the whole
Forgetting not Heaven,
he blesses Earth,
and even his smile illuminates the world.

*Source (75)*

Chapter 19

# Trust: The sweet jewel in the crown of Peace

I t is late... the sound of crickets at their chanting, a few flickering lights from cottages spread through the rice paddies in this enchanting land called Bali, where I sit at my desk before an open second-story window, contemplating Elohim's latest request to write on the theme of *Trust*. Well, the title leaped through me and onto the page, and so I will *trust* that something will follow...

★★★★★

My eyes fall easily on the soft glow of a new crescent moon. Abiding with this tranquil image, my mind gradually releases its incessant grasping until there is just a spacious emptiness. That is when, without any effort at all, I hear it: *the previously inaudible flow of my breath*... the s-s-s-s of an inhale, the h-h-h-h-h-h-ha of an exhale, and that delicious pause of silence between. That is when the mysterious 'it' hits me full force. In this case, the 'it' is the essence of this topic: Trust.

I cannot see or touch this mysterious life force that enters me with each effortless, unplanned breath. I notice that for the inhalation to occur, something within my body *opens to receive*. I am unable to catch the moment or intelligent mechanism that ends that receptivity, as the body briefly waits for an amazingly complex exchange of fresh life force and subtle waste matter deposited for curb-side pick up in my lungs, and then streams it outward invisibly into the cosmic recycle bin. What I have just exhaled, renewed mysteriously, will be inhaled in part by a multitude of living organisms. Perhaps these crickets will go on chanting...

What catches my attention is this sublime *'opening to receive.'* I am struck by this: is not the simple act of a breath a symbol of perfect trust? A willingness to open in this very body... and Life flows in. A smile emerges softly, and for a moment this crescent moon is a sentient messenger of the gods here just for me; carrying me into this moment of insight. Spontaneously, my favorite mantra arises in my mind: *Thank you, Lord, for my life. My life IS your Life; we are One.* It rises and falls a few times on the waves of this soft breath, then dissolves from inner awareness, and again there is only empty spaciousness, where sometimes still, I think an 'I' actually lives...

★★★★★

Along our way of the spiritual path, each of us must surely come to a place of reflection and meditation on this quality, verily, this Principle of 'Trust.' For as we begin to discern (at first, and for quite some time, like Alice: "through the looking glass") the deeper nature and requirements of this extraordinary alchemy that quickens our souls, illuminates our minds, heals our hearts, and transforms our hopes, dreams, values, and actions, it begins to dawn on us

*Spontaneously, my favorite mantra arises in my mind: Thank you, Lord, for my life. My life IS your Life; we are One.*

Baptism in the Jordan

that we are called to trust what 'eye hath not seen, nor ear heard.' Indeed, the Biblical prophet speaking in Proverbs (3:5,6) tells us:

"Trust in the LORD with all your heart; do not rely on your own thoughts."

"Wow, Nellie! Methinks we're not in Kansas anymore, Toto!" *Do not rely on my own thoughts???!!!* "Holy concepts, Batman! Just what do we do now???!!!" But Batman knows, and is troubled: it is just here we have unwittingly been led, not by our own unreliable thoughts, but by something else... something as mysterious as, well, as mysterious as this influx of life force that comes with a simple inhale. Here Batman stands, at the threshold to the very Kingdom of Heaven. Batman knows Christ stands on the other side, whispering:

"I stand at the door and knock. And to anyone who *opens and receives Me...*"

Hmmm, there's that little trick again! And just what will it take for Batman to open the door to the knock from someone unseen? Why, trust, of course!

Kansas, or heaven, Toto? With tail wagging, Toto saunters off down the yellow brick road, but will Batman follow him and Dorothy? It's not by accident that 'Dorothy' is a female; every religion and philosophical system regards the capacity to trust as a characteristic of the feminine energy, *Sophia,* divine wisdom. That is why religion has been a major preoccupation of *men* throughout at least the last 5,000 years: men have to deliberately grow the capacity of the feminine soul...

Batman is the symbol of the separate and wary ego-self here: he wears a mask (persona) and a costume designed to impress himself and everyone else! If he opens the door, he will become transformed under the gaze of Christ into the Emperor who wears no clothes. Why, he won't even be able to rely on his own thoughts anymore! And so he (we) stands, hesitating... hesitating... worrying, doubting, conflicted, *fearful,* and gripped in fear, that the mysterious mechanism and intelligence just can't work its magic, the magic by which we may *open and receive* and — in the wise words of St. Paul — be transformed in the twinkling of an eye.

★★★★★

It's been over thirty years since I left my own Kansas, there in the ordinary world of dreamers, called by something as invisible and ungraspable as this unseen sea of life force my body opens to with every inhale. They have been years spent cultivating an ever-deepening capacity for my very soul to *open and receive* as easily and effortlessly as this body — after much diligent work in Yoga and LovesBreath training — does with an inhalation. It is even more difficult for the soul than the body, until you get the knack of it, in which case its ease becomes habitual; its value, priceless.

I have come to see that virtually all forms of spiritual practices – from the precious ways of Yoga to the contemplative rituals of Tibetan prayer beads, from the reflective study of sacred texts to the critical feeling of core emotions, from radical and ruthless self-inquiry to the daily and humble confession of my ignorance and fallibility – all forms of spiritual practice are really about melting Batman's fear of being unmasked; they are really about flowering the capacity to trust: to *open and receive*. And can this be anything but the willingness to be reborn in a Love of all things as the presence of the Divine, right here, where once there was only a sniveling, whining, doubting being filled with the fear and futility of trying to rely on its own thought, it's own meaning of what Is, and Ought To Be? Methinks I hear that ancient prophet droning on and on: '...Do not rely on your own thoughts.'

And so, I want to share with you to pay attention: **Trust is what we are called to (re)learn here.** Indeed, it can be seen as our *only* purpose. For as this capacity slowly flowers (and it is a slow and steady movement, punctuated with blissful quantum leaps, in a field of monumental, complex and subtle resistances in body, mind, and soul), it brings about a radical transfiguration of the very soul that has answered the Call to the spiritual path; the one who ends this journey will not be the one who began it.

Trust undoes our own thoughts, those very things from which we construct a 'reality' we are so sure we see 'out there.' And, if you could see how profound this illusion is, it would blow your circuits (unless you have patiently learned with all mystics to open and receive the higher octanes of Light). Trust leads us inevitably to speak in agreement with Ralph Waldo Emerson:

*"All that I have seen teaches me to trust the Creator*
*for all that I have not yet seen."*

★★★★★

The good news is that Trust isn't just some ephemeral thing you decide to do without knowing how to do it, and thank God for that! Trust is *learned*, like any other skill that, when mastered, flows along of its own accord as we play on the notes of the divine song of Life. Whether through breath and movement, as with Yoga, or through inquiry, as with good counseling and facilitator's seminars; whether through study of the masterful teaching-wisdom of the Jeshua material (*The Way of the Heart*, etc.) or *A Course In Miracles*, we can all (re)train the flow of conscious impulse *away* from fear and all the forms of its contractions in mind, soul, and body, and toward and into this oh-so-precious capacity to *open and receive*.

We cannot even begin to comprehend just what this will change, and to what degree, but we have the word of countless Masters that it is certain to do so, and that this transfiguration is what we have desperately been seeking **by anxiously relying on our own thoughts**... deep, eternal, everlasting Peace – a peace that forever surpasses the world's understanding (for the 'world' is the effect of a distrustful dream), a peace in which Love is increasingly free to flow through this temporary conduit of flesh and mind we once mistakenly took to be 'me, and mine.'

It is here, when the work of God's Love into and through us has shattered the very roots of the dream of the dreamer itself (that thing we mistakenly identify with, called 'I'), that Batman, standing naked before the grace-filled, healing gaze of Christ-Presence, learns the secret of secrets, and I cannot find better words to describe this radical transfiguration than those of Al-Ghazali, a hugely important mystic from the Sufi tradition. He writes in his *Divine Unity* that – through a final and sudden mystical apprehension that comes and does not leave – trust finally blossoms and bears the sweet jewel that feeds us the elixir of Peace when one sees with startling clarity that:

*"...all that exists in creation – sustenance given or withheld, life or death, riches or poverty, and everything else that can be named – is solely initiated by, and originates in, GOD."*

It is from this level of highest apprehension, or Christ-Mindedness, that a master like Jeshua can teach us:

*"There are no wrong turns, nor 'accidents,' and only Love can be real. All things are but God's way to reach into your dreams and awaken you from the Dream of Separation, restoring you, according to your dreaming, to your rightful place in Creation: Christ. Unlimited forever, before all things, the very eternal thought of Love, in form."*

★★★★★

The crescent moon has disappeared without my even noticing it. But I have learned that the further I die into God's infinite presence, the more I notice how little I notice; paradox of paradoxes. I can withdraw attention from this body and visit a student anywhere, anytime, and commune with them; I can see the roots of a soul's karmic threads. These and many other gifts come

> *Trust in the LORD,*
> *indeed, by learning*
> *to surrender every*
> *grip of resistance*
> *to simply what*
> *IS, without any*
> *reliance on your own*
> *thoughts, and heaven*
> *will open to you,*
> *as it must.*

unbidden as one places one foot in front of the other, making the pilgrimage to the Heart of God. They, and all gifts, are only for His use, not ours. Yet, here I sit late at night at this desk, humbled by the fact that the last thing I remember was staring at the sublime beauty of a crescent moon. And now it is gone, and I didn't even notice! There is just this s-s-s-s-s of each inhale; the h-h-h-h-h-ha of every exhale, all of it happening of itself, and everything is of itself, *just so.*

I know this may sound radical, but enlightenment *is* radical: God's in His heaven (right here in every 'here,' right now in every 'now'), and all's right with the world. Yours and mine, right here, right now. So, go ahead, stop grasping and striving. Just *open and receive* this moment; this eternal, radiant, spacious, and radically free moment, for you are only the power to be aware, and just this is the breath of Life that is your life. Trust in the LORD, indeed, by learning to surrender every grip of resistance to simply what IS, without any reliance on your own thoughts, and heaven will open to you, as it must.

Go ahead, let all your attention be focused on taking the jewel of Trust in hand, this extraordinary and radical Trust, and complete your crown of Peace.

*What is it that is holding me back right NOW, in this moment, from moving into complete TRUST, complete allowance and complete acceptance?*

# Stepping Stones #6

*It is very, very important to let each day be sufficient unto itself.*
*That is, when you end your day, always truly end it.*
*As you take a deep breath, as you rest your head upon the pillow,*
*look upon the whole day, embrace it with your consciousness,*
*and as you let your breath go out, say within your consciousness,*

*I release and forgive this day.*
*It has been perfect. And it is done.*

*Let it go, just let it go...*

*Look upon the things of the day and say:*
*"It is very good. And it is finished."*

*Let each night, when you rest your head upon the pillow and you*
*know you are about to go off to sleep, be just like God was in the*
*story, your Biblical story of creation, in which it is written that on*
*the seventh day, God rested. God was finished, in a sense, within the*
*story. And have that same quality at the end of each of your days.*

*Source (76)*

Beloved friends, *I* come to where *you* choose to be. And if you would choose to open that place within the heart and within the mind in which you can communicate with me directly, I will meet you there as well.

*Source (77)*

You were birthed to be grand. You were birthed for greatness. You were birthed to shine forth such Light into this world that the world remembers that Light is true, and darkness is illusion.

*Source (78)*

Rest assured, then, that whenever you believe you have not succeeded or not completed some decision, fueled by desire, it is because you were simply not *wholly committed* – or it means that you decided to change your mind.

*Source (79)*

That freedom is what you abide in *always,* from before the foundations of this world, and long after this world ceases to be. In each and every moment, then, you cannot be a victim of what you see, and nothing is outside of you. What you experience you have directly and deliberately called to yourself.

*Source (80)*

The eye of the needle that separates you in your consciousness from the world of conflict and fear and guilt and unworthiness – that world and the world of the Truth of the kingdom lie side by side, within your own mind.

*Source (81)*

God simply never deviates from desiring
only the extension of Love, the birthing of
that which is like unto Himself – you. And
your will is joined with your creator's when
you decide to birth only that which reflects
Love – the good, the holy, the beautiful.

*Source (82)*

Photography by Michael Flatt

Chapter 20

# Dawn

The first traces of light dance faintly against my eyelids, and this body is stirred to waking. Where does the light end, and the eyelids begin? Where is this point of communion, this marriage that births the child of waking? Have you ever tried to find it?

I am still. I rest in that place just prior to the tendency to ignite the mind in thoughts – those little abstract mini-creations bubbling through the neuronal pathways of the physical brain that literally create a whole world immediately experienced, but affecting a buffer between pure awareness and this light making love with my eyelids, stirring the birth of this child I call 'waking up.' And is this not what we define as 'becoming conscious of my "self"'? And is not this self exactly the constellation of thoughts by which I define my "self" and thus become (re)oriented in space-time? Do you see?

The "self" does not become aware of where it is in space, it defines what *is* in both of two critical ways: time, and meaning – this constellation of thoughts whirling about in the brain, as light impulses "re-construct" our sense of self, and thus, construct the limits of what we know: behold the arising of the 'world'!

We do not see that even this constellation rests on a foundation of prior constellations, resting on a foundation of prior constellations, resting on a foundation of prior constellations, each more subtle and prior level even more 'ingrained'; that is, energy impulses 'grooved,' and more or less stable, like the pillars of a building. Inside the building, we may shuffle the furniture about endlessly, and easily (we call it new experience, and we are hungry for it when attention flows outward into the 'world'), but deep within and under the building, the pillars become few, and very substantial. If they were to shift, the whole building would shift. If they collapsed, the whole thing would fall down.

> ~
>
> *The soul is not the ego,*
>
> *nor even the bodymind,*
>
> *yet it pervades these,*
>
> *and is really the life of*
>
> *them, yet gets enmeshed*
>
> *with them.*
>
> ~

The ego fears this, because the ego is the building we have constructed: that familiar thing that re-constructs itself every morning, giving that felt sense of 'me.' The soul is not the ego, nor even the bodymind, yet it pervades these, and is really the life of them, yet gets enmeshed with them. It is more subtle, a much finer 'substance' (it really isn't physical at all, but in a physical world – including the lower mind – you must speak the language that can have some hope of being understood). Like the soft note of the oboe in an orchestra, it is usually drowned out by the horns and violins and drums.

And the soul yearns to break through, and be free of, the constant re-construction of 'me.'

The soul knows and feels Communion. At its level of being, it delights in the fact that the light and the eyelids don't really "end" at all, but merge and emerge in Wholeness, or Oneness. They are like two ends of a straw. Just try to have one without the other!

For, you see, soul is really Soul: that field of awareness that actually pervades all of Nature (and beyond, high and low). 'The earth is my body, and all that arises within it, I AM.'

That statement will seem astounding to the ego. It is self-evident when the seat of Identity has broken through to the first level of Soul. It can hardly be called 'one's own personal and private soul,' can it?

And if that is astounding, just wait to until you realize that Soul enfolds domains far above and far below Nature, too! It becomes only a thin strand of possible domains, like domains within domains within domains; pearls on a string within pearls on a string, within pearls on a string...

This is why it is futile and painful to take anything personally. There is no such thing, and thus nothing that can possess anything. Where there is really no substantial 'me,' there can hardly be a reason to justify the grasping of the ego, shouting 'mine'! This is especially true about the one thing the ego truly thinks it has: its own life. In truth, there is no self that has a life. To realize this is to fly beyond the realm of suffering, even though life continues.

Now this light grows in the eastern sky, turning cloud edges to gold and pink. Just how does one color become another? Does anyone really know? We could come up with some explanations: the gods are weaving magic in the sky. Molecules appearing as moisture build-up are being struck at progressive angles, and this changes the way the eye and brain formulate images and colors. Magical thinking, scientific thinking. Thinking, period.

And, as I mentioned, thoughts construct a new world of experience. Would you like your coffee with milk, milk and sugar, or just black? Behold, choose! And enter a new world!

~

*The one thing the ego truly thinks it has: its own life. In truth, there is no self that has a life. To realize this is to fly beyond the realm of suffering, even though life continues!*

~

I rest, here, just before the habitual tendency to enter the doorway marked "thoughts that will (re)construct my most familiar world, orienting a 'me' in space, defined by my thoughts about time (especially the time span of this particular body) and the meaning I have ascribed to its events" – especially the meaning I have given the really personal events that groove my deepest sense of a 'me.'

*Yet even that arises in the larger field of the Soul, that knows there is no such thing as a personal person.*

At rest, just now. Attention moves toward silence, not reconstruction theory. Mount Agung, Bali, emerges as darkness gives way to this light that marries my now-opened eyes, birthing something that has never been before this moment: a bodymind sitting in a chair being penetrated by a mountain at just this angle, this moment, this unique set of all-encompassing conditions far too vast to comprehend.

But more. As I rest, I notice the bodymind is being pervaded by the mountain. At a subtler level than reconstruction, there is no 'me' looking at the mountain. I can feel it – a very real energy pervading me, like 'coming on' to a medication or 'non-prescription drug,' or like those moments of really great sex, or falling in love (or is it, opening in love?).

If I allow a soft breath, yowza! It circulates quickly. I can witness it literally pouring into every cell. There! It just made it into the outer edge of the fingernail of my little finger on my left hand. Delicious, this! Blissful, this! The breath seems to allow the mountain to titillate every cell, penetrating more deeply. I am lover being penetrated by the beloved mountain.

Now, the mountain reveals itself to me. I am 'inside' it. I see beneath its surface to its core, like travelling within it, until there is no trace of a 'me' looking at the mountain.

There is only the Soul of the mountain arising. The Soul of all manifest things, arising, just so. Sacred Into-Me-See.

And so a simple principle of Life reveals itself. When I rest just prior to the need to reconstruct my world, I may be penetrated. When I am, I know the thing intimately. It is a knowledge that operates in a way quite different to the way 'knowledge' operates inside the tiny (re)constructed world of 'me' – that is always a knowledge 'about,' but is not the thing in itself, not a knowledge by being the thing known.

> ~
>
> *There is only the Soul of the mountain arising. The Soul of all manifest things, arising, just so. Sacred Into-Me-See.*
>
> ~

If you have ever had a very-first-time-experience, like of chocolate or sex or a rock-n-roll concert, you know perfectly well what I mean, don't you? There is knowing that transcends all knowing 'about.' That is why there's nothing quite like the first time! And why there is no sense trying to get it back! Lucky for us, if we could only get it: Every moment is the first time, always.

Stop living in the constant (re) construction of 'me,' like the pillars and floors of a familiar house in which you know where every room is, and what is inside them already, so that you merely keep repeating entering and leaving, leaving and entering, ad nauseam, like a record stuck in the same old groove. You know, the thing you always insist is 'my life.' It is merely a (re) construction act you do habitually every morning when the first touch of light of what could be a whole new day caresses your eyelids, and you leap, not from the bed, but from this prior Soul into the world of 'me'!...That very little, spellbinding world in which knowledge "about" things is taken to be the same as knowledge "of" things.

Like this knowing, and being known by, Mount Agung. This merging dance of light, of being, arising just now.

I have learned that by resting prior to the habit of Reconstruction, perhaps with a friend, with a mountain, with a paper cup, or with someone wanting to heal and awaken, and even with things that are not present objectively, this deeper Knowing may occur effortlessly. Knowledge by Being is like making love with... Infinity.

Yes, I still look at things. Yes, the reconstruction arises, but it has no glue, no spell-binding power. In fact, manifest existence, including this morning sunrise, and the mountain, and you, are felt to be arising within a circle of awareness whose center is everywhere, and circumference nowhere!

If that confounds you, don't worry. Just want true wakefulness, and it will come to pass. For what truly IS just loves to undermine the pillars of the house of 'me,' collapsing the limits of our construction so that what IS can show itself off!

There is a word we use to describe this thing that IS, beyond – yet pervading – our tiny constructed world of 'me.' And the word is 'God.'

~

*There is a word we use to describe this thing that IS, beyond – yet pervading – our tiny constructed world of 'me.' And the word is, 'God.'*

~

Is it a benevolent personal old man with a grey beard? Yes! If there is any mind aware of God in that way, then Yes!

Is it a complex of energetic patterns defined as E=MC squared? Yes! If there is any mind aware of God in that way, then Yes!

Is it a stern taskmaster? A stream of Grace? Is it non-existent?

*Yes! Yes! Yes!*

*And that is what makes God, God, isn't it? Everywhere you look, there it IS, for it is the very power that allows all looking, all seeing, and is yet forever hidden from final view.*

Until you finally turn around in the very seat of the soul, and let the gaze of awareness penetrate to the real Soul of the perceiver itself. "Peek-a-boo! I see You!" – God shouts, and reveals itself to be the power by which all things are seen, just as you damn well choose to see them. As a mountain 'over there,' or a mountain 'arising here.' The big thing 'over there' is much, much bigger when it is allowed to 'arise here,' inside the perceiver!

Now it is palpable for me. So self-evident. There has been no separate self at all! The emperor has no clothes because there is no emperor! The entire universe, no, the entire Kosmos arises within what was always Me, squeezed to the unseen edges of awareness when once I fell under the spell: the spell of the habit of Reconstruction Theory.

I saw, really saw into and through, how I did that with every judgment, every unforgivingness, every fusion of identifying my 'self' with the choice to stamp things with 'me, myself, and especially, Mine'!

Consider this for yourself – and learn to cease grasping, owning, craving, needing – and God will emerge in the Gap of your resting, resting into each Moment in which only the New is arising. Yet the silence in which it is occurring is undisturbed.

~

*Give up the habit of reconstructing everything with the spell of Me-Myself-and Mine. Just stop, that is all. Just rest in the space prior to that habit. Let God emerge.*

~

Give up the habit of reconstructing everything with the spell of Me-Myself-and Mine. Just stop, that is all. Just rest in the space prior to that habit. Let God emerge.

I have been reduced to three ways to describe God, this palpable, self-evident Isness:

As the field of energy eternally dancing as all temporarily arising things, God is the Ever-Shimmering One.

As the intimate source from which I and all things arise, I am aware of a feeling-quality that can only be Love, and so God is the Infinite Beloved.

And in the humbling recognition that there is no finality I can ever achieve in knowing or being known by That One, I must cease all arrogance and rest in the utter unknowability of God. And, thus, God is "Hashem," a Jewish word that means: beyond name and form.

Precisely in these three qualities, I am at rest in the Home of my Creator. Abiding thus, only this can arise: surrender in devotion, a tear of gratitude, and a subtle movement constantly in my heart compelling this temporary swirling of molecules we call a bodymind to be used to help others out of their Reconstruction habit, to taste the golden wine, this nectar sweet above honey!... the literal, immediate, palpable taste of God.

And now the sunlight is warm on the skin, for the first time.

A thought arises and its pleasurable currents begin to mobilise these molecules to leave this desk and come to the edge of the pool next to my cottage. There I will remove this sarong, and let the warming sunlight kiss this body. Then, step into velvety waters.

For the first time.

For all things are being made New every Moment. Only this can be the meaning of Presence in the Eternal Now.

It is not a concept, theory, or belief. It is Reality, waiting on your welcome – if you are willing to take up that PathWay that dissolves the habit of identifying with Reconstruction Habits! The only glue holding the habit in place is a fear, or recoil against the Real Thing Actually Occurring: God. Here, and Now. Beyond illusion. Palpable. Infinite. Bliss-full.

You have squeezed yourself into a tiny box of Me–Myself–and–Mine. Rest prior to this habit, and become the Freedom you already are. Give up the ghost, and die into this life divine.

We'll do lunch, praying love in God.

Come and abide in Me. Come and drink of this Presence that has made its Home where once these molecules were also recoiled in fear through the habit of constant Reconstruction Theory. Be quickened in My Presence, dissolving in Grace the glue of Me–Myself–and–Mine, and be exploded into radical freedom.

Here, there is only astounded Wonder, simple Innocence, and extraordinary Infinitude. Joy. And the final Peace when nothing is obstructed, or recoiled from. There is only the recognition that the only thing occurring, ever, is God Praying Love in, through, as, and for all things. Including you.

Abide in Me, and be Free.

Would you like your coffee with milk, milk and sugar, or just black?

*Ask yourself: "Where can I step forward with greater boldness from this day forth?"*

# You are Home

So you see, in the end, it is not so much about
cutting out certain experiences and having only
certain ones that you've decided hold value.
It is, rather, to see that all such experiences
are transitory. A moment of ecstasy or a
moment of sadness are one and the same for
the Enlightened Mind. There is only that Vast
Expanse that allows all things.
And when nothing is any longer unacceptable
to you, in the field of what seems to be your
own unique, particular experience, you will
know that you are Home. Things arise and pass
away, and you remain.

*Source (83)*

# The Closing Word

S omething magnificent awaits us all. Yet, it is not so much a *thing*, as much as it is a *remembrance*. Yet, this remembrance is not simply a memory. It is like what happens when we lift above the clouds and are stunned by the shimmering beauty of sunlight, unobstructed, radiant, unlimited.

It is like what happens when we forget ourselves completely, as the beauty of a dolphin's leap from its hiding place in the ocean takes our breath away.

Only, in this case, it gives our real breath back to us.

It is the breath by which we feel the Divine coursing through us as the Life of our life,

And the very Soul of our very soul.

This awakening is the province not of religion, for – as Carl Jung pointed out – religion is really a defense against what we zany mystic types, having found our way above the clouds of the ordinary world where the dolphin has given us back our real breath, spend the rest of our lives attempting to describe and (if we are so called by the Beloved One) attempting to challenge anyone daring and willing enough to strap in for the ride of their life *to* the source of their very Life. That is, this remembrance is an awakening to genuine religious experience: everywhere, suddenly, all things shimmer in divinity, as though a spell has been broken, as though a dream has dissolved and with it the very dream of the dreamer itself.

Make no mistake about it. Enlightenment is very real. It isn't the kind of thing you can debate, or even choose, for it is the destiny of every soul to awaken. In this, there is no choice. *When* we are moved to submit to the Fire that purges us of illusion is the only choice we really ever have.

Regardless of all our dreams, our strivings, our judgments, fears, and reasons, eventually each of us must take up this universal pathway and be taken above the clouds of this dream world.

~

*A genuine spirituality is not a bed of roses, at least for the ego! It progressively shatters the roots of fear, of specialness, of hope for getting things to go our way, and of our very resistance against acceptance of Who we really are.*

~

But I do not speak of going anywhere else. For the Real World shimmers, *here*. Not as we have thought it to be, nor as we might wish it would be so that our egos may be satiated, but as what alone Is, has Always Been, and forever Shall Be.

There is simply no way anyone can be convinced of this radical notion, nor can we know Reality conceptually. It is not a matter of belief, or of disbelief. There is only one way:

To take up the pathway whereby we awaken from the grip of the Imposter, the false and limited self.

A genuine spirituality is not a bed of roses, at least for the ego! It progressively shatters the roots of fear, of specialness, of hope for getting things to go our way, and of our very resistance against acceptance of Who we really are.

It carries us from myopic intimations of what love is, into Love itself.

It changes everything – *everything* – for it changes the very seat of the soul itself. And when the seer is finally undone, all things finally appear as they truly are: liberated in joyous innocence in the lap of God.

Imagine no sense of lack, nor fear of loss. Imagine capacities of awareness that the clouds of our ordinary mind have kept hidden, blossoming to reveal the subtleties of all things. Imagine feeling no sense of separation from a single being or expression of Creation.

Imagine a peace so pervasive it enfolds all tears in gratitude. Ordinary mind cannot even begin to wrap itself around the very non-dual, palpable, self-evident marvel that the Mystery of the Divine really is!

Yet, to awaken, we will first come to be confounded, pissed off, and challenged in ways we could not anticipate. But death of delusion comes on no other road but this.

The journey of true awakening requires a few things in our cosmic backpack:

Courage, vigilance, discipline, yes. But more than these, it takes us through territory that can only be traversed with constant forgiveness, constant willingness, a surrender of all hope for control, and an increasing capacity for laughing at the futility of the ego to ever win!

And above all, it requires this: *faith*.

And faith — if allowed and followed faithfully (no matter what) is the experiment that becomes the experience; the direct lived experience of a genuinely awakened being.

When it is time, you cannot prevent the path from seizing you altogether. When it isn't time, there is nothing you can do to get on it, or stay on it, for, at the first bit of rocky terrain, fear will seize you rather than love, and fling you back below the clouds, and you will mutter how crazy it was to even think there was a way to the dolphin beyond the clouds.

In the end, the essential requirement of the mystical journey is the willingness to die and be re-born altogether in the deepest bedrock of the soul. The first part of the journey is a journey *to* the Kingdom. Then, and only then, comes the journey *within* it. And no one, *no one,* knows what this is until the seat of the soul is transfigured.

Faith is the willingness to submit to what is unseen, unheard, and unknown. It is the willingness to discover what it really means to let go, and let God.

I hope these parting words confound you a bit. It's necessary, you see!

There is really nothing I, nor any mystic can do, to persuade you of the Real World. You must come to see it immediately and directly for yourself. Except, if you make this journey, the one who comes to see the Real World will not be the one who set out to find it!

For, to 'see' requires *new eyes*. A genuine spirituality is the art and science and grace that transfigures the ability of the soul to see, first. And few there be who are truly willing to submit to such cosmic surgery.

Perhaps you will be one of them. Perhaps not.

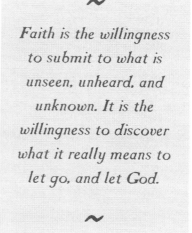

*Faith is the willingness to submit to what is unseen, unheard, and unknown. It is the willingness to discover what it really means to let go, and let God.*

As for me, there is so much more of God to surrender into! My final whispered advice:

God is an ocean of infinite depth and width.

Sail on, dive deep.

Be utterly shattered and die as many deaths in one life as possible. And be sure to die *before* you die, so that — at death — you will not die yet again, only to be born again in the misery of *samsara*, slowly moving to the very conditions in which you can Choose Anew; to the very conditions in which you find yourself as you read these words... now!

Go ahead. The whole universe is waiting to support you, as it does at all times, even if you choose illusions and the ordinary world there, beneath the clouds.

*Go ahead. Die into this Fire and be free. Dare to discover what it means to let God become the Life of your life.*

It all begins with a little willingness, and ends in infinite, eternal Mystery. All I can promise you is this: it will have been worth every price paid as the false self is made burnt toast, and the hosts of heaven celebrate your return to your rightful place.

But since you have, and never will have, a clue as to how to get there, remember this simple key, and use it often: prayer.

Pray not for things, nor for solutions to perceived problems, but pray without ceasing that you be awakened from every last trace of belief you have ever been separate from God.

Let the Grace Stream have its way with you. Just pray for this, and submit.

This is enough. This is all.

Now, I have a date with unseen silence.

Blessings,

**jayem**

*Jewels of the*
CHRIST MIND

"Masters have always seemed as though
they are just a little bit crazy.
So, let yourself become even crazier!

Become a fool for the love of God.
For who will perceive you as a fool
but those who are taking
themselves seriously?

And why would you continue to pander to
the minds of the insane?"

*Jeshua*

*When we truly become fools for God – having seen that the
world has not nor ever will offer anything of value –
we will give ourselves over to transformation without end,
so that two things can occur:*

- *We are kissed more deeply by the warm lips of the Divine*

- *The Divine might pour out through us to bathe this
suffering world.*

*The soul that is truly awakened lives not for itself,
for it sees there is no such thing as a separate self called 'I.'
The soul that is truly awakened lives not 'for' anything,
but 'by' the shimmering Presence of the Divine.*

*Source (84)*

# INDEX

## Sources for Inspirations and Quotes

(57) Selection – Jeshua Teachings

(58) Selection – Jeshua Teachings

(59) Selection – Jeshua Teachings

(60) Selection – Jeshua Teachings

(61) Selection – Jeshua Teachings

(62) *Way of Transformation* – Lesson 11

(63) *Jewels of the Christ Mind*

(64) *Way of the Heart* – Lesson 1

(65) *Recline in my Soul*

(66) *Way of the Heart* – Lesson 12

(67) Selection – Jeshua Teachings

(68) Selection – Jeshua Teachings

(69) Selection – Jeshua Teachings

(70) Selection – Jeshua Teachings

(71) Selection – Jeshua Teachings

(72) *Way of Transformation* – Lesson 2

(73) *Jewels of the Christ Mind*

(74) *Recline in My Soul*

(75) *Way of the Servant* – Book 2

(76) *Way of the Heart* – Lesson 3

(77) Selection – Jeshua Teachings

(78) Selection – Jeshua Teachings

(79) Selection – Jeshua Teachings

(80) Selection – Jeshua Teachings

(81) Selection – Jeshua Teachings

(82) *Way of Transformation* – Lesson 9

(83) *Way of Knowing* – Lesson 9

(84) *Jewels of the Christ Mind*

*It is with deep appreciation that the following Friends of the Heart are acknowledged for their contribution in birthing 'Cosmic Chocolate Orgasm.'*

Barbara Theis

Susan Jones

Michaela Richter

Corinna Stoeff

Sophia Fils

Jennifer Bertram

Caroline Leonard

Sally Carter

Diana Prowse

Barbara Brewster

Darma Qi

Gene Thompson

Hetty Driessen

Alan Shrimpton

Kate McNamara

Katarina Bereza

Margaret Taylor

Lisa Thompson

Josephine Snell

Pamela Rosalynde

Eylan Rose

Eppe Keizer

Dave Schock

Joy Poulter

Marianne Bateup

# The Way of Mastery PathWay

The PathWay offers a comprehensive roadmap if you have the desire to **grow, heal** and **know** yourself truly.

It includes **five core texts, additional materials** and a series of alchemical **living practices** which offer support that ideas alone cannot achieve.

## The Five Core Texts

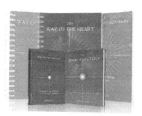

1 ~ *The Jeshua Letters*
2 ~ *The Way of the Heart*★
3 ~ *The Way of Transformation*★
4 ~ *The Way of Knowing*★
5 ~ *The Way of the Servant*

★Also available as the original audio.

## Living Practices ~ additional material

*LovesBreath, Radical Enquiry,* the unveiled original teachings of *The Aramaic Lord's Prayer* and *The Aramaic Beatitudes,* meditations including the much-loved *In the Name,* together with the in-depth darshans of the Online Ashram—these are all key elements of the PathWay.

## Living Practices ~ insight groups, workshops, retreats and pilgrimages

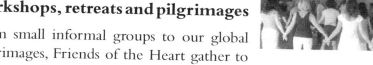

From small informal groups to our global pilgrimages, Friends of the Heart gather to grow together.

You can find out more about the PathWay and all that it offers by visiting our website, where a wealth of video and audio excerpts, and much more, awaits you:

**www.wayofmastery.com**

Made in the USA
Lexington, KY
25 November 2015